LIVING IN PARADOX

Lettie,
Life is a game,
Play consciously!
All the best,

LIVING IN PARADOX

Perspectives of a Refugee
Made in America

Phong Le

LIVING IN PARADOX, Perspectives of a Refugee Made in America.

Library of Congress Control Number: 2006907545

ISBN: 978-0-9789046-0-9

First Hardcover Printing November 2006

Available at WWW.LULU.COM

Dedication

To Madison and Devin

"Memory is the fabric that connects all of us"

-- Mark Twain --

Acknowledgments

I am indebted to all my friends and family for their assistance in recalling countless memories and helping me organize my thoughts

I am grateful to my kids, the key inspiration to record my life memories, so they will never forget their heritage

I wish to thank my Editors for their skillful handling and valuable suggestions to make this book fundamentally human. Special thanks go to Stan Bert, Marsha Campbell, Patrick Dennis, Dr. Steven Howe, Boriana Ilieva, Kenny Leung, Oanh Nguyen, Kristi Overgaard, and Ellen Simonetti

I owe a general acknowledgment to all the people that I have encountered for sharing their stories and allowing me to observe their performance on this stage called Life

Lastly, I am most grateful to live in America, the Land of Opportunity where everyone has the right to pursue Life, Liberty, and Happiness as defined in the Declaration of Independence

Contents

Prologue 1

The Journey to America 3

From Rags to Comfortably Set 15

6° of Separation 43

The Business of Sex, Love, and Marriage 69

The Search for God and Spirituality 93

Finding Balance 107

Next Steps 123

Prologue

It has been at least 5 years since I've had an extended vacation and I'm beginning to feel burned out from toiling with startup companies. Business is good, very good, but my passion is beginning to fade. I decided to take a break to travel more and recap my life to reveal clues to where I'm heading next; thus the initial inspiration to write this book.

At first, I thought that I was too young to be writing about my life, as I'm only 40 years old. But then I realized that I've experienced a great deal more than most people would in a lifetime. I began grappling with the notion of the daunting task of recalling countless memories that are unique to me. Having lived in America for more than 31 years, I pondered if those memories are even worth sharing. I never thought I was capable of writing a book, much less a book about myself. I've been approached by many asking to write a story of my life, so what better time to start than now.

My journey began when I was 9 as a refugee fleeing war-torn Vietnam for the Land of Opportunity. Through hard work and with a great education, I began pursuing the American dream. I adapted to a new culture. I survived the sharks of the business world and made a comfortable life for myself. I survived falling in love, or the perception thereof. And most importantly, I survived the insanity of searching for God and my Spirituality. Along the way, I've met some very interesting people and collected many wonderful memories which will forever be imprinted in my mind.

The chronicles to follow are part biography, part spirituality, with glimpses into the business of entrepreneurship, gambling, sex, love and marriage, and ultimately, self-enlightenment. My story is only one of the many perspectives of life's little secrets, based on the experience of a refugee pursuing the American Dream. The tale about to be told is direct and to the point and is true to the best of my recollections. Names have been changed to protect the *not-so-innocent.*

The objective of this book is to inform and educate those interested in seeking the truth in order to better understand our contradictory world. I hope you will find it entertaining and profitable. Learn some lessons since we will not live long enough to make all the mistakes ourselves.

Life is just a game, learn the rules, make new rules, enjoy the ride!

The Journey to America

The year was 1975, one week before the Fall of Saigon on April 30th. Under the cover of darkness, my family and I were rushed into a cargo van off to an undisclosed airport hangar. There we waited for a safe window at sunrise for the transport plane to take off. I was too young to remember much in the chaos and fear of being caught, but one lasting image was forever imprinted in my mind. During those hours, we were herded like cattle. I can still see myself cornered on the floor of the cargo airplane with my eyes fixated on the American soldiers mounting machine guns on the airplane windows to protect us. Then I fell asleep. There were much more horrific stories of people escaping on foot and by boats, but we were the lucky ones. Hours later, I awoke to a new world where my journey began.

For those not familiar with the Vietnam War, here is a bit of history. According to a documentary from PBS, the Vietnam War was the longest and most unpopular war in American history. For many of more than two million American veterans of the war, the wounds of Vietnam will never heal. Fifty-eight thousand Americans lost their lives and the losses to the Vietnamese people were appalling. The financial cost to the United States came to over $150 billion.

American involvement began in 1955 with the arrival of military advisors. The first combat troops arrived in 1965 and the war was fought until the cease-fire in January 1973. South Vietnamese leaders believed that America would never let them go down in defeat. This belief died as North Vietnamese tanks besieged Saigon on April 30, 1975 and the war ended with South Vietnam's surrender. As with any war, the political, economic, health, educational, and social disruptions were beyond description. The toll in suffering, sorrow, and turmoil was immeasurable.

I was only nine when my family fled for America, so my memories of Vietnam are sketchy at best. I came from a family of eight siblings, seven boys and one girl. From my recollections, our family was somewhat educated and we were sheltered from the war. I was educated in a Catholic school – a very strict environment where corporal punishment was common and encouraged by parents. I don't think I was a very good student, since I remember often having my behind spanked, my face slapped, and my knuckles whipped by priests and teachers.

Other memories were going to the beach house, riding around the city with my dad on his motorcycle, getting run over by a motorcycle, canoeing in the river to harvest vegetables, playing with marbles, swimming in the rain, competing in cricket fights, and camping. Another lasting impression was a spiritual ceremony I attended that incorporated a demonstration of body piercing, fire-walking, lying on beds of nails, tongue cutting, etc. I think it was more of a side show than a religious ritual. Then suddenly, all of our lives changed that one night when we were rushed out of the country and an entire new world opened for us. I recall that we were only allowed to carry one item, so I carefully packed my prized fighting cricket into a matchbox. More interestingly, my dad, a well known and respected educator in Vietnam, took only his guitar.

From Saigon, also known as Ho Chi Minh City, our first stop on the flight to freedom was in the Philippines to refuel, then onward to the very small island of Guam in the South Pacific. The indigenous people of the island are called Chamorus. Around 1678, Guam was colonized by Spain. It was later captured by the United States in 1898 and then occupied by the Japanese during World War II. After World War II it was returned back to the United States.

Until today, Guam is still a strategic location for U.S. military installations in the Pacific Ocean. At the time, Guam became the first of many locations to house the influx of refugees from Vietnam. Our family ended up staying in Guam for about three months to help with the settling of refugees. My only memories from the refugee camp are waiting early in line for food, watching movies under the open sky, climbing coconut trees, and being enamored by the jets and helicopters taking off and landing on gigantic aircraft carriers.

Next stop on our flight to freedom was the refugee camp at Fort Chaffee in Arkansas, with layovers in Hawaii and California. From the early days of World War II, Fort Chaffee was a key military training installation. In 1958, Elvis Presley was inducted into the U.S. army and began basic training there. It was also the location for the filming of the movies <u>Biloxi Blues</u>, and <u>A Soldier's Story</u>. In the late 1970's, Fort Chaffee was home to over 50,000 Southeast Asian refugees, including myself.

The only thing that stood out in my memory of Fort Chaffee was that it was very hot and humid. There was no air conditioner in sight. I remembered spending most of my time learning English and playing baseball. At Fort Chaffee, we waited and waited for our sponsorship papers to be processed and to be told the location of our new home in America. Then we were notified that a sponsor had been matched and we were cleared to move to Sweetwater, Texas to begin our new life.

Shortly afterward, we were on a flight to Abilene, Texas and were driven 45 minutes to Sweetwater to meet our sponsor. He was a man who owned the local Holiday Inn Hotel. With the sponsorship, he received free labor. In exchange, we had a free place to live until we found our own home and could sustain ourselves. Sweetwater is a small town in West Texas and in 1975 it had a population of about 10,000 people.

Today the area is known for Wind Energy, the world's largest Rattlesnake Roundup, and at one time, unfortunately known for being the capital of methamphetamine labs. Our family lived in Sweetwater for about 5 years. During those times, we were very much welcomed. We stood out everywhere we went, since most people in town had never met an Asian in person. Sweetwater was a very tranquil community. We adapted quickly with the help of the local churches and the welfare system.

Growing up in Sweetwater was quite a different experience from what I imagined America to be. For the first few months I was somewhat disappointed. The vision about America from Vietnam was much more glamorous. However, I was very eager to learn the language and culture. It was not easy starting over from the very bottom of society but we adapted. Everyone in the family who had the opportunity to work, worked long hours. We took advantage of every charity and accepted anything that the government could provide. We had free lunch passes for school and colorful money with which to shop. I remembered running to the grocery stores to buy food and it took a while for some cashiers to figure out how to process food stamps. We were on a very strict budget and I couldn't even afford to buy a flea collar for my stray dog.

My pre-teen and teen years in Sweetwater were a lot of fun. I did well in school, though I was often hanging out with the wrong crowd. We shoplifted for fun, marked the town with graffiti, and experimented with homemade explosives and rockets. Often we were out vandalizing, blowing up dumpsters, and chalking cars with eggs. Once we stole a riding lawnmower and took it completely apart and returned it to the owner in pieces. It seemed like good fun at the time. We frequently gathered at local videogame parlors to share the mischievous stories of the day and to plan our next target. Summer pastimes included playing baseball, tennis, fishing, hunting small game, hanging around the porch playing ping pong, and picking fleas off the dogs.

Another recollection of Sweetwater was the weather. It was hot, very hot. We still did not have air conditioning at home. Then came my first white winter. It was a most memorable day. My teacher called me out of class to take a walk outside and I was able to touch a snowflake for the very first time. I was in awe for the next few days playing in the snow, sledding down the hills, and building snowmen.

I was adapting quickly to the American way of life, living in a small town, making new friends and having lots of fun. Then we got the bad news one day. My dad was diagnosed with leukemia. At the time, leukemia was a mysterious blood cancer and there was no cure. He was diagnosed at a late stage and died a few months later, a few days before Christmas. He was only 46. We did not get to spend many years together but from what I remember, he lived life passionately. Being an educator, he was always curious and indulged in art, theater, music, history, languages. He made sure that each one of us received a great education, had access to art and music, and was involved in the community.

From his first savings, he bought the family a piano and he bought a clarinet for me to play in the marching band. I really wanted a guitar but there is no guitarist in a marching band. I kept the clarinet and became the first chair throughout school. He even enrolled me in Boy Scouts and I quickly became a squad leader. In Vietnam, my dad was well-known as one of the premier educators in the country and he even taught the son of the President of South Vietnam at the prestigious school of Lasan Tabert. The transition to the United States was very difficult for him. He did what he had to do to make ends meet by working at a cotton factory and in an electronics factory assembling parts.

During his last hours, he was too medicated to share his thoughts, drifting in and out of consciousness. I think he got what he needed from this life and he was ready to move on. Being only 14 at the time, I don't remember mourning for him much but I continued to see him in my dreams at happier places for several years after his death.

After my dad passed away, my mom was left devastated and with a lot of hungry kids. She struggled to make ends meet, working long hours for minimum wage in a garment factory. In search of a better life, she uprooted the family and we moved even further West to Lubbock, Texas. In Lubbock, my mom ended up working on the assembly line for Texas Instruments. Many years later, she took early retirement with the same company.

Lubbock is home to over 200,000 people today, relying on the vast agricultural and cattle industry in the area, as well as on a variety of manufacturing facilities. Depending on which way the wind blows, there is a distinct smell from these industries that can blanket the city at any given moment. Lubbock was also home to Mac Davis, Buddy Holly, and it was once called the birth place of tornadoes. The weather is very unpredictable since the city is located at an intersection of pressure systems. One year I remember we had a sandstorm, thunderstorm, tornadoes, and a snowstorm, all within a period of 4 hours.

What I remember most about the move to Lubbock is that we finally found a home with an air conditioner. It was also in Lubbock that our family finally received our United States citizenship which made us bona fide Americans. Lubbock is a great place to raise a family and to obtain a good education, since there is not much else to do in this flat area. The city is dry and you have to drive 30 minutes out of town to buy beer or liquor but that didn't stop most people.

Between going to school and working odd jobs, not much happened in my life while I lived in Lubbock. I focused intensely on getting good grades to prepare for college and I was on the honor roll throughout high school. I did take some time to play sports and I was very good at baseball and tennis. However, recreational time was limited as I was trying to make a few bucks on the side working at the local supermarkets and fast food chains. By the way, the five-second rule is well practiced in the fast food kitchen. Any food that is dropped on the floor and stayed there less than five seconds, can still be served to the customers.

Among my other exciting jobs were mowing yards, night janitor for a movie theater, and student teacher assistant for summer high school. It was an interesting experience teaching biology and math to drop-outs from regular high school. I learned a lot about why these kids were considered troublemakers. Most are really over achievers. Often they come from dysfunctional families and are under challenged. Without guidance, they became rebellious and ended up being a menace to society.

In America, having your own wheels is considered a symbol of freedom, to go wherever you want, whenever you want. I was ready for mine. Up to that point, my means of transportation had been sharing a ride by car, bus, and bicycle. I was now ready for my driver's license. An odd thing happened though when I went to the Department of Public Safety to apply for my driver license. I brought my immigration papers with me as proof of identification, and for some reason, it had the wrong birthday. To this day I have two birthdays. The correct birthday that I celebrate and the legal birthday on my driver license and all my legal papers. I have to do some explaining every time I'm asked about my birthday.

Back to my wheels. Within a year of getting my driver license, I blew the engines on two cars, wrecked one, and wiped out on a motorcycle. The motorcycle accident left me with scars of pebbles along the right side of my body from head to toes. Needless to say, I was either having a string of bad luck or I was just careless. I think it's a combination of both. Luckily no one was seriously hurt.

As my last year in high school was winding down, I began planning for my college years. I was often told that education is the key to success and I took that saying very seriously. I was in the top 10% of my class, so I didn't have any trouble getting accepted to a major university. I applied to only two schools in Texas and I was accepted by both Texas Tech University in Lubbock and the University of Texas at Austin. Getting accepted was the easy part. Now I had to figure out how to pay for all this. I had no car, no money, so I began applying for student loans and grants. I received just enough to get started. My sister helped to choose my first used car and I was off to college in Austin, Texas. It was a good car for the price but it had a lot of electrical problems. There were almost no brakes and the door even fell off once. When it happened, I almost died laughing. I strapped the door with the seat belt until I made it to a welder to have it fixed.

On my first night at college in Austin, I slept on a park bench. The next day, I registered in a dormitory. A few days later, I went looking for a job and began working 20 hours a week while taking 15 credit hours of classes. Having to work long hours, taking many classes, and trying to have a social life, my grade point average suffered tremendously. The following semester, I was put on probation. Like everything else, I needed to adapt quickly to catch up. So I attended the University of Texas at Austin during the regular semesters and Texas Tech University during the summer when at home in Lubbock.

The college years were trying years for me, as I was on the road to discover myself. I changed majors three times, from Aerospace Engineering, to Accounting, to Business Management. I made a lot of great friends and socialized a bit too much. Being the Social Director for a student organization, it was hard to resist. I had the largest budget in the organization and planned or attended parties every weekend. Needless to say, I had my share of wild days.

Then there were the college roommates. I had some good roommates and some bad roommates. Kyle was my first roommate. He experienced being drunk for the very first time with my assistance in choosing six different brands of beer. We became best friends ever since. I also had a gay roommate and he was very open about it. He would put on tap-dancing shoes and follow me to the gym to workout. At the gym, all he did was practice tap dancing while every other guy in the room was pumping iron. At the time, homosexuality was still a taboo and I often overheard conversations with his parents who were trying to get him psychological help. Afterwards, he would break down crying, wondering what was wrong with him.

After the good, came the bad and the ugly roommates. To save money, I once roomed with 6 guys in a two bedroom apartment. Being guys, they were not very clean. We called our apartment the roach motel as every roach trap in the apartment was full. The place was filthy. The walls were often littered with markings of roaches smashed on the walls and left there. Obviously, we never got our deposits back.

Memories of my college years are quite a blur. Perhaps it was the alcohol or the hormones. It seemed that there was one party after another, one football game after another, and school was just getting in the way. It was the best time of my life, being so carefree with no thoughts of the real world. That false sense of security came tumbling down when it was time to graduate and look for a real job.

Lucky for me, my days of socializing paid off. As a result of my involvement with AIESEC, the world's largest international student organization, I found a platform to discover and develop my leadership skills. This was how I landed my first job out of college. I left for Europe for my job in Belgium before I had received my final grades. The thought of failing my last exam was so real that it was imprinted in my dreams. For years, I had nightmares about going back to college to retake my exam. A decade later, I did return to the University of Texas at Austin but this time it was for my Masters Degree. Now I have a second degree, a Master of Science in Science and Technology Commercialization.

Having been in Texas for more than 31 years, on and off, I'm positively a Texan. When traveling abroad, I'm often asked where I'm from in America. As soon as I mention Texas, most everyone will reply with "*Are you from Dallas*" or *"Do you know JR?*" The TV show Dallas put Texas on the world map, as did the Dallas Cowboys and both Presidents George Bush and George W. Bush. Texas is also well known for championship teams such as the Dallas

Cowboys, Dallas Mavericks, Dallas Stars, Texas Rangers, San Antonio Spurs, Houston Rockets, and Houston Astros. And we must not forget the University of Texas Longhorns, the 2006 College Football National Champion.

Much more so than its sports teams, I think Texas is best known for its sheer size and for being the Lone Star State, the diversity of its people and landscape, as well as the rich heritage and hospitality of its residents. I have traveled to many places around the world and no matter where I go, Texas will always be home.

The difference between Vietnam and America is vast, even more so when compared to West Texas. It's ironic that I'm here in America because of the Vietnam War. War is nothing short of devastation but it is also a chance to start over. The United States is the only country in the world that I know of where a person can start from the very bottom of society and with hard work and a solid education, can be anything they are determined to be. Sometimes change is good. My journey was just beginning.

From Rags to Comfortably Set

Fresh out of college and in debt, the chase for the American dream was set in motion, starting in Europe with U.S. based companies. My first real job was in the French side of Belgium in the city of Liege. I began as a management trainee with Unisys Corporation. A year later, I moved to Rome, Italy to take a post as a management consultant with Peat Marwick, which is now KPMG. These were great positions with lots of flexibility which allowed me to jump on a train every weekend to discover a new European city or country. Regarding the languages, I adapted quickly. Within 6 months, I was dreaming in French and Italian, and I was able to converse.

Coming from West Texas, I was a bit naïve. I experienced my first major case of culture shock on a camping trip with a group of college students. When it came time to change clothes, I quickly noticed that there were no separate rooms for boys and girls to undress. Everyone disrobed in the same room, at the same time, without hesitation. That was a nice shocker for me, so I played along.

Later, I learned that most of Europe is very open-minded and nudity is no big deal, as most beaches are topless. Other cultural differences that stood out included having to pay to use a public toilet, having to pay tolls on every highway, public transportation that was fast and cheap, and that tipping is included in all your bills. Great food, great wine, and great music are integral parts of everyday life in Europe. I was treated very well by all.

There was only one unpleasant experience on my way back to the United States. I was mistaken for carrying a bomb by the Italian police and that was not fun. They tore apart everything I had. This was a time of rampant terrorism running in Europe. I should have expected the suspicion since I had to walk past two security guards armed with machine guns everyday to get to my office. However, I did manage to bring back a beautiful handmade replica of a 300 year old Belgian shoulder bow designed for war and elephant hunting. This bow weighed 30 lbs. and it was made for me as a gift by one of only three shoulder bow makers alive at the time. I enjoyed my time in Europe immensely. I grew considerably and expanded my cultural horizons during my brief stay in Europe.

After Europe, still broke and carefree, I made my way to New York City and landed a position at Citibank as a Trust Officer managing investment funds. They say if you can make it in New York City you can make it anywhere, and I did. Living and working in New York City is a symbol of capitalism at its best. I was hot on the trail to pursue life, liberty, and happiness, but all I found was work, work, and more work. At first, I had a great time exploring the city, making new friends, but somehow I got sucked into the rat race. At one period, I didn't get to feel the sunshine for 6 months. All I remember was that a car service picked me up and took me from home to work and vice versa, day after day.

I worked long hours and saved enough to make my first and worst investment buying land in central Florida from a friend. Never saw the land but I trusted my friend. I eventually sold it 12 years later only managing to break even. In a way, I felt robbed but that doesn't compare to the time I was caught in a gang shooting in Chinatown, or the time that I was mugged, and that was a funny incident. You haven't experienced New York City till you have been mugged. Everyone in my circle of friends in the City had been mugged.

My mugging incident began on a return trip from Dallas, Texas. I took the subway home and as soon as I reached street level, I was jumped by two men who were after my wallet. We struggled for about a minute on the street and we rolled around the gutter with cars honking and driving around us. No one stopped to help. Needless to say, they got my wallet and ran. I was lucky to be alive. As I was gathering my things, a lady came up to me and said, "*How come you didn't use your karate on them?*" I looked at her bewildered and left the scene.

Not all Asians know karate and it would be several years before I would receive an award for rookie of the year and two black belt degrees in Martial Arts. There was another time when a guy at a bar tried to pick a fight with me and I turned to him and said, "*If we get into a fight, I'm going to tickle you to death.*" Hearing this, he laughed and bought me two rounds of drinks. A little humor always helps relieve the tension in any situation. There was so much anxiety brewing in the area that one time the city adopted the motto "*Don't worry, Be happy*," and stickers began popping up everywhere.

After 3 years in New York, the city was beginning to get to me. The noise, the pollution, the crime, and the division between the rich and the poor became too much. I woke up one day and decided to return to Texas. I had made great friends and contacts in New York. If you happen to be in a certain sports bar in the Upper West side with two tennis trophies behind the bar, you will find my name on them. I donated the trophies after winning a charity tennis tournament two years in a row. New York was a great experience and I left my mark there.

Moving back to Dallas, Texas! It was great driving across America. Even more so when I saw the skyline of Dallas and suddenly I felt home again. Once settled, being a driven individual, I couldn't wait to start my next project. I knew that I was a quick learner and could do anything, so I dabbled with various projects and began focusing on job training. I networked my way through and helped to launch computer training programs for the Federal Bureau of Investigation (FBI). Then I moved onward to virtual reality training for a new surgical procedure called laparoscopic, a micro-invasive surgical technique which minimized the incision size and greatly reduced the recovery time after surgery.

To learn more about surgery training, I followed a group of surgeons as they attended weekend courses to get certified for the new procedure. Certification for this new surgical procedure was usually done by operating on live guinea pigs. Sometimes there was a shortage of guinea pigs so the pigs get operated on again and again. It was not a pretty sight and many mistakes were made. The guinea pigs were destroyed humanely afterward.

During these training sessions, it struck me that there must be a better way to train a person for any skill set. Current programs were ineffective and expensive. I began researching for new tools and soon afterward gathered the right talent and funding to launch Creotec, a multi-media training company. At the time, it was a new concept to provide an audio/video CD-ROM based on an interactive informational environment, equipped with stills, motion video, and continuous audio in multiple languages. We were featured in numerous magazines and newspapers including the *Dallas Business Journal, Technology Review, Amiga World, New Media*, and *CD-ROM News*. We were way ahead of our time.

However, our efforts did not catch on until a decade later. Our navigational tools and similar menus are now found on every opening screen of a Digital Video Disk (DVD). Many lessons were learned from this venture, particularly that the best technology does not always win. The up side though, was that my network continued to grow and I used that platform to begin helping other entrepreneurs bring their ideas to fruition.

For the next few years, I continued to seek out ground breaking technologies, consulting with multinational companies like EDS, TXU, MCI, and Verizon on various projects while dabbling in the Stock Market. The market was on fire then and everyone was making money. Greed was running rampant and everybody wanted to become a Day Trader. I invested well, left it to grow, and decided to go back to graduate school. A few years later, I received a Master of Science in Science and Technology Commercialization from the University of Texas at Austin.

Then I took off to Brazil to relax and plan my next project. Brazil was fantastic. It is one of the few places in the world where the locations are more beautiful than the postcards. I almost did not make it back alive after being caught in the middle of a human stampede at the national championship soccer game. It was a scene straight out of CNN. As I approached a crowd at the stadium, suddenly all of them came charging at me followed by riot police on horseback, galloping and shooting people down with rubber bullets. Then the police fired shock grenades into the crowd, pursued by police dogs chasing and chomping down any stragglers. Anyhow, I made it back unscathed and I was ready for my next project.

Next stop, Los Alamos. Through a connection I made in graduate school, fate brought me to Los Alamos, New Mexico. Los Alamos is world famous for one thing. It was the location of the Manhattan Project, the secret 1940s mission to design and build an atomic bomb. Two atomic bombs were produced at Los Alamos, nicknamed Fat Man and Little Boy. The ones that devastated two Japanese cities, Hiroshima and Nagasaki, forcing Japan to surrender less than a month later and ending World War II. Over the years, Los Alamos National Laboratory (LANL) has become one of the largest multidisciplinary, multi-program research institutions in the world.

In addition to nuclear science, LANL has developed capabilities in areas such as supercomputing, information management, advanced materials, sensor technologies, biosciences, earth/environmental sciences, etc. LANL is also credited as the birthplace for the human genome project which was initially focused on the study of genetic mutations caused by radiation. Another invention from LANL impacting our society was the TollTag, which allows us to zip through the tollbooth without depositing coins.

Living in Los Alamos was a somewhat surreal experience. I was surrounded by intellectuals, natural beauty, and one of the clearest skies. I took advantage of the opportunity and was often found star gazing with powerful telescopes from the local astronomy club. Here I was, deep in the mountains near the base of a volcano, surrounded by a beautiful landscape, and this was also the birthplace of the atomic bomb. There was a joke circulating during World War II and the Cold War with the former Soviet Union that if any employees at LANL were asked, "*What are you guys making up there?*" they would answer, "*Oh, about $3.35 an hour.*"

Initially, I was brought to Los Alamos to help launch the world's first nanotechnology incubator which involves the manipulation of matter and antimatter to produce new materials, structures, and devices. The applications to be developed ranged widely from nuclear medicine imaging, to antiproton cancer therapy, to antimatter rocket propulsion. This was my first time being exposed to the world of antimatter.

The history of antimatter began with a physicist named Paul Dirac back in 1928. Dirac wrote an equation combining quantum theory and the theory of relativity, which later won him the Nobel Prize in 1933. But the equation posed a paradox. Dirac hypothesized that for every particle that exists there must be a corresponding antiparticle exactly matching the particle but with an opposite charge. For example, for every atom there should be an '*antiatom*' identical in every way but with an opposing charge. That charge will annihilate into a burst of energy upon contact with ordinary matter. Thus, Dirac speculated on the existence of a parallel Universe made out of antimatter, separated by magnetic and electric fields.

It was not until 1995 that the answer was revealed when an antiatom was produced at CERN, Switzerland. Using a particle decelerator instead of a particle accelerator, scientists were able to force a positron (or antielectron) to stick to an antiproton making an antihydrogen atom, a real antimatter atom. Since atoms are the building blocks of matter, this experiment came a step closer to proving the existence of an antimatter Universe. It is very possible we all have a twin in a parallel antimatter Universe!

Based on this and other scientific discoveries, the nanotechnology incubator was formed. Nanotechnology is a field that promises the creation of molecular materials and machines. By manipulating individual atoms, scientists hope to create atomic micromachines to build supercomputers the size of atoms, or molecular robots that can destroy infectious microbes, patrol our bloodstream to remove bad cells, engineer cheaper and safer foods, clean up hazardous wastes, etc. It is even more exciting and equally startling that there is a belief that these molecular machines may be able to reproduce on their own and become self aware.

Originally, the nanotechnology incubator was a venture backed by Ted Waitt, founder of Gateway computers and a billionaire at the time. Nonetheless, the venture was politically challenged from the start and it never fully materialized. Lucky for me, I was later introduced to the folks at the technology commercialization office at the Los Alamos National Laboratory (LANL) and I came on board as a venture consultant.

At LANL, I was engaged in identifying breakthrough technologies and matchmaking scientists and investors to launch startup companies. Being a science fiction fanatic, there was no better place to be than in the middle of the research at LANL. I was like a kid in a Willy Wonka's chocolate factory. I entertained breakthrough ideas and experimented with prototypes for robotic insects, artificial intelligence, non-invasive brain scanning, biosensors, genetic engineering, nuclear medicine imaging, nuclear powered battery, nuclear rockets, quantum computing, virtual reality, electric airplane, zero emission energy, etc.

It was very difficult to draw the line between which technology was real and which was science fiction. Most scientists think that their ideas are the best and only need some funding to prove their concepts. And at the same time, potential investors wanted to see ground-breaking, disruptive technologies, and they wanted a return on their investment in one to three years. It was a challenge to satisfy both parties but I did manage to bring a few ideas to fruition and in turn provide a platform for my next project.

Things were going well with my efforts at LANL and my network kept expanding. Then something unforeseen happened. Another cycle of war was about to begin. On the morning of 9/11/2001, I was having breakfast at home when a breaking news bulletin flashed on CNN. I couldn't believe what I saw. The headline 'Attack on America' was on every channel, and like most people I could not get a call through. I sat in silence and was dazed for several hours watching the live events unfolding.

Shortly afterward, LANL was on high alert and everything changed as paranoia settled in. Additional security personnel were called in and barricades were erected at every key building. For the next few months, there was little activity at LANL. Access became restricted. At the same time, the Stock Market was already weakening. The tragedy on the morning of 9/11 hastened its decline and it took a steep dive. The Federal Reserve Chairman, Alan Greenspan, warned about the exuberant market months earlier. The tragedy of 9/11 just accelerated the bursting of bubbles, one after another. I was being affected financially and personally, so I decided to place every commercialization effort on hold until the fog cleared. Nevertheless, I continued to travel to LANL from Dallas, Texas to maintain my relationship with high level officials.

A year later, I received a call from my friend Larry Calton. Larry was one of my contacts who was part of an entourage I led from Dallas to LANL on earlier efforts in technology commercialization. Everything was about to change again. A few months earlier, Larry was contacted by the economic development team from the City of Frisco to launch a Center to help fledging startups in the area. At the time, local industries and the job market in the Dallas/Fort Worth area were in a slump and talents were beginning to leave for greener pastures. The airline industry, the telecom industry, the software industry, all the backbone industries in the area were devastated after the stock market crashed. On the other hand, certain retail markets continued to do well and the center of that resided in the City of Frisco, a suburb of Dallas, Texas.

With new tax dollars pouring into the city, local leaders came up with the idea of a mechanism to grow their own companies. They needed a theme. A feasibility study was done and a new industry was recommended for the area. It suggested that existing technologies and talents in the area could be combined to build a medical technology corridor. Hence, the North Texas Enterprise Center for Medical Technology (NTEC) was born.

The mission of NTEC is to assist entrepreneurs with starting and growing new medical technology ventures. The Center provides a broad base of support to select entrepreneurs, both internally and through its extensive resource network. NTEC is supported through a public-private partnership between the Frisco Economic Development Corporation (FEDC) and Hall Financial Group, and by a contributor network of Stakeholders. With Larry on board as Executive Director, he needed a director with the technical and business background to help kick start the process. That was where I came in.

From the day I engaged to the day I stepped down, we were going at mach speed. It was literally a ground-up operation with no time to waste. We all had to wear many hats. We designed the facility from its foundation up and watched the idea become a reality. Wall by wall, room by room, it began to take shape. The equipment and furniture began to fill the rooms. I remember the first day we moved in and all we could hear was ourselves echoing from one corner to the next.

Three years later, the center was 95% occupied and billion-dollar markets were being created by our entrepreneurs. Expansion plans are in the works to build a facility four times the existing size where NTEC would be the anchor tenant in the first of many buildings in a new medical technology park.

I like to think that our success was due to having a good process in place, a strong network of advisors and volunteers, and an executable plan. Launching a startup is still as much an art as it is a science. However, if you start with the right tools, a lot of mistakes can be avoided. NTEC was a gamble for the City of Frisco and for all of those involved. We hope to cash in soon to help more entrepreneurs bring great ideas to reality.

TEN QUOTES FROM ENTREPRENEURS I ENCOUNTERED:

"The idea came to me when I was sitting in a casino playing with a condom"

"This new innovative procedure is painless, no more pain than a root canal"

"Our technology is so advanced that we do not have any competition"

"We only need to capture 1% of the market and we'll be rich"

"My garage blew up last night working on this new formula"

"With $100 million we can make this work"

"I cut off my finger yesterday trying to put this prototype together"

"I can't believe you meet so many people with better ideas than mine"

"I need money for my own business and I don't see why I can't have it"

"My technology is so compelling, so revolutionary that it will change the world, but I can't tell you what it is"

I'm often asked, how do you determine which idea is worthy of nurturing and investing? We try to keep it very simple, often known as KISS (Keep It Simple Stupid). Once an entrepreneur is selected to present to our advisory team, they are required to provide a presentation covering the following areas:

- ***Product overview*** – What is the product or service and what are the key factors that make it unique or innovative?
- ***Pain and Solution*** – What is the pain and how will the product or service solve the problem?
- ***Customers*** – Who are the target customers and what are their needs and requirements?
- ***Market*** – What is the market size, growth, achievable market share, and the window of opportunity?
- ***Product development*** – Where is the development state of the product or service, prototype, and its scalability?
- ***Distribution and sales channels*** – What are the channels to reach the customers?
- ***Competition*** – Who are the competitors and what are their key characteristics and differentiators?
- ***Competitive Advantage*** – Design a competitive matrix to show competitive advantage and barriers to entry.
- ***IP*** – What is the likely Intellectual Property (IP) protection for the product or service?

- ***Financials*** – How will money be made, assumptions, reasonableness, and return on investment?

- ***Funding requirements*** – How much money is needed and how will the funds be used?

- ***Alliances and Partnerships*** – What relationships have been established that can add value to this venture and what is the status of those relationships?

- ***Management Team & Board of Directors*** – Who is on the team and what skill sets do they have to address the launch?

- ***Milestones*** – Illustrate a time line to identify critical milestones achieved or to be achieved along with the use of funds.

When assessing a venture, at the onset, we collect the basic information from the categories above to determine whether the product/service is better, faster, cheaper, and whether it is scalable. Then the due diligence process begins for validation of the information presented. If the overall consensus is positive, then we extend an offer for the entrepreneur to join the Center. The full breadth of NTEC services is then implemented to accelerate the process to commercialization. In essence, NTEC acts as an interim management team, for a small equity position in the company.

Managing a startup is like running a marathon but at the pace of a 100 meter dash. It is the ultimate balancing act because the target keeps moving, so you have to continue to improvise and adapt. There are certain gaps that need to be filled before a company goes out raising capital, as they may only get one shot at pitching to an investor. These gaps are sometimes referred to as the 'Valley of

Death.' By identifying the gaps in the early stages, we can determine how much time, money, and resources it will take to bring an idea to reality.

Even though it may be a great idea, this is still a business and we have to ask ourselves, how will these products save time and make money? It is the basic mentality in the business of WIIFM (What's In It For Me?). It's an ongoing educational process for all.

The biggest mistake that I often see is a failure to plan or underestimating the competition, whether it is out of fear or just plain laziness. Time and again, I see great ideas but with no action plan. Most entrepreneurs tend to neglect the competition, thinking that no one has thought of this idea before. That is their Achilles heel. For me, the number one thing that I look for in any venture is 'who the competitors are and what prevents them from doing the same.' To be more efficient, know your competitors and respect your competitors, as your competitors can also be your partners.

There is one NTEC story that I would like to share as a classic example of a successful startup in the making. The story began three years ago, when I received a call from Julian Ross, founder and CEO of OxySure. Julian was looking for office space and assistance in bringing to market a ground breaking medical technology that would revolutionize how medical oxygen is delivered. He had developed a process and methodology to generate medically pure oxygen from two proprietary inert powders. At the time, it was a one-man operation working out of the garage. When Julian and I first met, it was not so easy to see where OxySure was going but now the path is clear.

Envision medical grade oxygen in a lightweight portable cartridge or pouch. This technology makes the provision of medical oxygen safer, lighter, and less expensive than traditional compressed oxygen cylinders systems. The upcoming products will improve access to emergency oxygen that affects the survival, recovery, and safety of individuals in two multi-billion dollar markets involving both established and expansion customer markets: (1) Individuals at risk for cardiac, respiratory, or general medical distress needing immediate help prior to emergency medical care arrival; (2) those requiring immediate protection and escape from exposure situations or oxygen-deficient situations in industrial, mining, aviation, military, or other public settings.

NTEC's decision to admit OxySure to the program was more than just it being a cool technology. We saw an entrepreneur who was fully committed emotionally and financially, and most importantly, an individual who was very coachable. As a result, after three years at NTEC, significant milestones were achieved. OxySure now has a production ready prototype cleared by the Food and Drug Administration (FDA) for over-the-counter sales with no prescription required. Top research institutions have validated the technology. A portfolio of intellectual property has been filed in the United States and worldwide. A stellar management team and boards have been formed. Key partnerships have been established with suppliers, manufacturers, and distributors, and customers are in place.

All of these components have contributed to OxySure's ability to attract considerable capital. Its accomplishments are a testament to NTEC and OxySure's commitment and determination in positioning OxySure to achieve tremendous growth and to make a great impact on society. The OxySure products are expected to be available in the market by March 2007.

After more than 3 years at NTEC, it was time for a change again. On March 1, 2006, it was announced that I was appointed to the Center for Space Nuclear Research (CSNR) as an International Liaison. It was a big surprise for most everyone in my network.

When the news came out, one of my investors called and said, "*Congratulations, I didn't know you were that smart*." I wasn't sure if I should take that as a compliment. I have always been fascinated with space travel, so when the opportunity arrived to rejoin a long-time friend and collaborator, I couldn't resist.

A few months earlier, a good friend from Los Alamos, Dr. Steven Howe, was appointed Director of CSNR. Dr. Howe and I chatted about possibilities, and a post was created. This is more of an ambassador position. It will allow me to continue to explore new opportunities in cutting-edge research while continuing my commercialization activities in collaboration with NTEC. In addition to space propulsion, the CSNR and its affiliates and partners would also be addressing medical technologies and applications necessary for the expansion of the U.S. space program. As in the opening comment of Star Trek, space is the last frontier. And there are riches to be made in the space adventure.

According to an article in *Business 2.0* magazine entitled, '*The Entrepreneur's Guide to Outer Space*,' the space business may be the most incredible new opportunity of our lifetime. Worldwide government spending on the space race is soaring to $50 billion a year, with the National Aeronautics and Space Administration (NASA) representing only $16 billion of that total. In the next 20 years, NASA is likely to sign contracts for as much as $400 billion for a human mission to Mars.

In addition, the private-sector spending on space applications now exceeds government spending as billionaire entrepreneurs like Richard Branson, Jeff Bezos, Paul Allen, Elon Musk, and John Carmack have been backing space-related companies for years. In the coming years, suborbital tourism, space hotels, and bases on the Moon and Mars will all become a reality.

As I'm writing this book, real-estate billionaire Robert Bigelow, head of the world's newest orbital space program, successfully launched the first of many inflatable modules for a private-sector space station, setting the foundation for the road ahead to human orbital flight.

Since its inception in 1958, NASA has accomplished many great scientific and technological feats. Most notable milestones are the lunar landings, unmanned missions to all the planets in our solar system, the creation of the space shuttle program and the International Space Station, as well as countless satellite launches to enhance life on Earth.

Moving forward, NASA has even more ambitious milestones to achieve. From an excerpt of a speech given on August 2006 by NASA Administrator Mike Griffin, NASA is charged to carry out certain specific programs including the returning of Americans to the Moon no later than 2020; launch of the Crew Exploration Vehicle by 2010; increase knowledge of the impacts of long duration stays in space on the human body; and enable humans to land on and return from Mars and other destinations.

The programs are extensive, however, space exploration is simply cost prohibited for any single nation. Outlays for these megaprojects are soaring. International cooperation on such projects is of the essence. NASA is becoming more open to cooperation from the international community including the European Space Agency, Brazil, Canada, Russia, Japan, as well as a number of Asian-Pacific countries.

In a recent article on *Space.com* entitled, '*NASA Chief Prepares for China Visit*,' scheduled for September 2006, Administrator Mike Griffin will be the first ever at the NASA government level to visit China to discuss space cooperation. China is the third nation to have the means of sending humans into Earth orbit. The former Soviet Union accomplished the feat in 1961, followed by the United States in 1962 and China in 2003. China is also a major player in launching satellites for a wide variety of purposes, including weather-watching and Earth remote sensing.

By 2012, China space planners will be landing a rover on the Moon's surface. By 2017, that country's lunar exploration plans call for robotic lunar sample return missions, followed by a manned mission to the Moon. This time, our race back to the Moon is not with the former Soviet Union but instead with China.

In addition, plans are already in the works at NASA for the colonization of other planets in the next few decades. According to NASA, since 1961 more than 400 human beings have ventured into space. Now aboard the International Space Station, astronauts are working to improve life not only on Earth but also to extend life beyond our home planet. It is inevitable that we will run out of resources here on Earth or be destroyed by natural disaster. Space colonization is not just speculation but a matter of survival for the human race.

The funny thing about watching the evolution of space exploration unfold is that I have a photo taken of me in a space suit while visiting NASA a few years back. My daughters brought the photo to school for a show and tell day. Later we got calls from various mothers to see if I was really an astronaut. Well, maybe one day I can be.

In the meantime, I look forward to taking some time off for travel, hobbies, and to do some volunteer work. One volunteer project for which I'm allocating more time is the Prison Entrepreneurship Program (PEP). Since May 2004, PEP has engaged the nation's top business and academic talent in an innovative solution to constructively redirect inmates' skills and energy by equipping them with value-based entrepreneurial training, enabling them to productively re-enter society.

After the security clearance was obtained, I made my first trip to the state penitentiary in July 2006 at the Hamilton Unit in Bryan, Texas. I was among a dozen executives invited to evaluate business plans for specific ideas that are feasible to pursue once the prisoners are free. The inmates conceived the ideas based on former work experience. With the help of MBA candidates from universities, research materials, data and statistics unavailable from the inside were provided to complete the business plans. Then business leaders, like myself, are brought inside to evaluate these plans. When I arrived, I could feel the energy and nervousness from everyone gathered in the room. The experience for me was a cross between a boot camp and a pep rally.

Participants in the PEP program are carefully screened. To garner a spot in the program, inmates must endure an intensive application package, including a completion of a 23-page questionnaire. Inmates must demonstrate ambition and they are held to high standards with rules, consequences, and accountability. "*Here are guys who are already seasoned entrepreneurs, who as drug dealers, for instance, already know about competition, risk management, profitability*," says Catherine Rohr, founder of PEP and a former venture capitalist. "*Teaching them passion is not something we have to do. What we do is show them how to make it legit.*"

In addition to studying core business subjects, the inmates are exposed to training in basic life skills. With knowledge, tools for earning a living, and continued support on the outside, the rate of recidivism should plummet. Currently more than 90% of PEP participants are in jobs. Studies show that of former inmates who are rearrested, 89% do not have jobs. It costs about $3,700 for one inmate to finish the PEP program, compared to $22,000 a year to keep him locked up.

PEP is one of the best causes I have seen in years. Its impact is life-changing for the executives and the inmates. Thomas Jefferson once said, "*If you want to learn about a society, study how it treats its prisoners.*" While I can, I'm donating my time and expertise as Executive Judge for the Prison Entrepreneurship Business Plan Competition, and will partake as Executive Mentor for recently released inmates. It has been a pleasure to be included in the program and I hope to see it expand nationwide. Perhaps, PEP could even be made into a TV reality show.

Beside the volunteer projects and being an encyclopedia for technology trends, I plan to keep a close eye on the progression of innovation around the world for commercialization opportunities. The United States is still the dominating force in technology and innovation but the rest of the world is catching up fast. According to a report in *Newsweek*'s International Edition, much of the concern centers on the erosion of science and technology in the United States, particularly in education. We are beginning to lose our competitive edge.

Recently, the National Academies of Sciences, Engineering, and Medicine issued a report arguing that the scientific and technical building blocks of our economic leadership are eroding at a time when many nations are gathering strength. The National Academies' report points out that China and India combined graduate 950,000 engineers every year, compared with 70,000 in America, and that for the cost of one chemist or engineer in the U.S., a company could hire five chemists in China, or 11 engineers in India. In addition, out of the 120 billion-dollar chemical plants being built around the world, only 1 is in the United States and 50 are in China.

Nonetheless, there are some encouraging signs. In a recent report from *Inc.com*, in the early 1980s there were just 270 entrepreneurship courses offered at colleges and universities across the nation. Today, there are roughly 5,000 courses available and some 200,000 students are now enrolled in some type of entrepreneurship class. Entrepreneurs who tend to start companies are younger and younger.

Now more than ever innovations are needed to solve problems confronting our society such as poverty, over population, health epidemics, energy, global warming, terrorism, etc. History has demonstrated that when new inventions are introduced into a society the society changes for better or for worse. This can be a major problem for the United States if we can't adjust to those changes. For me, where there are problems, there are opportunities, and we have little choice but to adapt quickly.

So, what does the future of technology entail? We are living in a very unique time in human history when knowledge is growing exponentially. Ideas are becoming a reality faster and faster as technology becomes more and more efficient. For example, the Human Genome Project, one of the most ambitious projects in medical history to decipher the genetic makeup of a human being was finally completed in 2003, after 13 years and billions of dollars spent. In the next few years, you will have your personal DNA decoded in just a few minutes for pennies. Analyses of the data can be used to develop techniques to reprogram your DNA to eliminate diseases and maybe even reverse the aging process.

In an article in *American Scientist* magazine regarding aging, through various diet and genetic manipulations, scientists were able to double the lifespan of laboratory animals such as mice, fruit flies, and worms. Similar approaches might help human beings stay healthy longer.

Technology is advancing at a dazzling pace and we are approaching a crossroad. This crossroad is the convergence of nanotechnology, genetics or biotechnology, and the integration of human and machine. Examples of how these technologies are currently being implemented in our society include stain/wrinkle-free khaki slacks, transparent sunscreens, cloning (i.e. Dolly, the cloned sheep), genetically modified foods, genetically engineered drugs, gene therapy, artificial muscles, artificial hearts, bionic arms and legs, cochlear implants, neural implants, memory implants, etc.

In the near future, it is possible we could create a new race of humans with superhuman intelligence and superior survival abilities.

Are we ready to control technology? Technology has great potential to improve lives around the world. Nevertheless, technology is a double-edged sword and there are many consequences if society is not ready to adopt it. If we can avoid being destroyed by our own invention, barring any natural disaster or unforeseen forces, we can utilize technology to truly be masters of our own destiny.

THE ICING ON THE CAKE

I wasn't sure how to incorporate the next topic but sincc it is related to making money, this is as good a spot as any.

A few years ago, through trials and tribulations, I discovered a way to beat the casino. I was never one to leave things up to chance, especially when it's within my control. This is the time when I used statistics to test the gambling establishments. Vegas anyone?

I've always had a gift for identifying loopholes. This gift I applied to the casino industry. At first, I questioned whether gambling is a game of chance or a game of skills. In my research, I found that the casino industry was expanding faster than ever, particularly on Native American reservations. These casinos were quickly outpacing the ones in Las Vegas and Atlantic City. The majority of the casinos were rolling in money. The average return on investment in the casino industry is about 15%, year after year.

This was a very good business to be in, both for the short term and for the long term. This told me that casinos were engineered to provide a consistent source of revenue over time. This was no game of chance for the casino owners. On the other hand, was it a game of chance for the players?

Gambling does not have to be a game of absolute chance. There is a secret strategy to winning in gambling, and I'm debating with myself about sharing this strategy, since it could tear into the fabric of the casino industry. I am concerned that if this strategy is implemented by the players many jobs will be lost, and the casino industry will probably change the rules to these games. After careful consideration, I decided to only share the basic strategy.

Everyone knows that casinos are built on losers and most people who gamble expect to lose money in the long run. Well, I never bought into that attitude. Over the years, I have figured out how to dramatically increase my chances of winning at most games and with a certain game you can beat the casino legally. Even Mark Cuban, billionaire founder of Broadcast.com and owner of the Dallas Mavericks, believes professional gamblers are a good investment, so much that he announced a gambling hedge fund to invest in professional gamblers. He looks for gamblers with a confirmable track record and hires them. Well, I didn't wait to hear from Mark Cuban to be motivated.

Over a period of 7 years, I developed a winning strategy and it has been refined over the years based on pure statistics rather than on luck. Luck for me is when you have at least a 50/50 chance of winning. But in a casino, there is not a single bet where you have a 50 percent chance of winning. The games are already rigged for you to lose over time. Nevertheless, if you only place bets with the highest odds of winning at the time of the highest probability to win, you can increase your odds of winning to 80 percent.

Since 1998, I have accumulated numerous data points and have put my strategy to the test at more than 30 casinos, with over 1,000 hours in simulations and live playing time. The strategy is very simple. Study the rules for each game and choose a game or bets that you're not required to play every hand. Every game and every bet in the casino has a payout ratio. Monitor each game and place only bets with the lowest payout, at the moment in the statistical pattern when you have the highest probability to win. The lowest payout bet is the bet where you will have the highest odds of winning. At the intersecting point of the lowest payout and the highest probability to win, if played consistently, eight out of ten times you will win. It is possible to beat the casino.

If you are disciplined, and if you can stick with the strategy over time you will win. How much you win will depend on your bankroll and how well you manage your money over time.

In addition, I recommend gambling only at casinos that are publicly traded and in states with a gaming commission that enforces frequent and unannounced inspections. Unfortunately, cheatings do occur among casinos and players. Case in point, while testing my strategy in a casino in Shreveport, LA, my mobile phone kept going off but there was no incoming call. I suspected cheating was going on so I called the state gaming commission in Louisiana the next day.

To my surprise, I was told that they only have two inspectors on staff and they only make unannounced inspections twice a year. Since that experience, the only place in the world where I feel the casinos and players are kept in check is in Las Vegas, Nevada.

There is one more factor to determine whether you are ready to gamble to win, and that is discipline. Discipline is the key in gambling because there are many distractions from too much alcohol, beautiful women, curious bystanders, and the dealers themselves trying to throw you off of your rhythm.

I usually try to limit my playing time to stay focused and to not attract too much attention, as I have been asked to leave a casino before. If everyone played the same strategy that I have developed, the casino would go broke. For me, it's just fun to beat the casino and recover the expenses of the trip. Maybe I'll write a book on this subject in more detail in the future.

So, for a refugee boy, I think I've done well for myself and this is just the beginning. I have a comfortable life. However, making money was never my motivation, it was only a means to an end of attaining wisdom.

Making money is one thing, keeping it is another. Money is power. Knowledge is power. Time is power. All of them are interchangeable with their negative and positive implications every time we make a decision.

True success usually comes from failure. This is the paradox that we live in as we try to reconcile our daily decisions to attain our needs and wants. What I've learned is that you have to live smart and economically, and you must practice moderation. Make an effort to live consciously and you will have the power to control your own life.

I've enjoyed all the opportunities that exist here in America. Should anyone really want to succeed, they can't help but have their dreams come true in this country. If you have the right attitude and recognize that anything is possible, there is a silver lining in every challenge.

> ***"An average mind talks about people,***
> ***a good mind talks about events,***
> ***a great mind talks about ideas"***
>
> -- Eleanor Roosevelt --

6° of Separation

We are all connected. There is a theory that anyone on this planet can be connected to any other person on the planet through a chain of friends that has no more than five links. The theory was first proposed in 1929 by the Hungarian writer Frigyes Karinthy. That theory is often referred to as the six degrees of separation. For me, it is more like three degrees of separation.

Over the years, through my business dealings and personal travel, from Luxembourg to Belize, to Brazil, to China, it has become obvious how we are all connected. On one trip, I met a man that used to work for a former business partner of mine. On another trip, I met a woman that grew up in the same small West Texas town where we made our first home in the United States. At another juncture, I met a woman whose uncle provided one of my best friends' sister her first job. It's obvious for me, I don't have to look very far to see the connecting links.

As a result of business, hobbies, and travel, my network has grown exponentially. My Rolodex is probably my most valuable asset. By leveraging the network, I can get just about anything done, from tapping into high-net-worth individuals, to gaining access to high level officials and CEOs of companies, to obtaining VIP passes via the gate keeper. I try to keep notes on everyone that I have been introduced to and I visualize what it is like to walk in their shoes. This is my way of networking where I find a common ground to connect.

As a connector, I have an aptitude for bringing together two parties with shared needs and wants. To illustrate how small the world can be, below is a list of a few people that I have encountered in my journey. Some of them are dear friends, some I have been just briefly introduced to. They are all connected and recognized at some level within the national or international community. Their links are also my links within this chain of the six degrees of separation:

- Buck Revell, former Associate Director of the Federal Bureau of Investigation (FBI), the Bureau's second highest position. In 1987 he was placed in charge of a joint FBI/CIA/US military operation which led to the first apprehension overseas of an international terrorist. He received presidential commendations from Presidents Reagan and Bush, received the FBI Medal for Meritorious Achievement, and was awarded the National Intelligence Distinguished Service Medal by the Director of the CIA. Buck has a book titled, A G-Man's Journal: A Legendary Career Inside the FBI - From the Kennedy Assassination to the Oklahoma City Bombing.

- Lt. General Jack Woodmansee, Jr., Ret. Jack served in Vietnam commanding helicopter units and flying over 1500 combat hours. He is the recipient of multiple distinguished service awards including the Distinguished Service Medal (2), the Silver Star, Distinguished Flying Cross (5), and the Cross of Gallantry with Palm (Vietnam). Jack is a former White House Fellow, served as a National Security Fellow at the Hoover Institution of War,

Revolution and Peace at Stanford University, and was an Assistant Professor of History at the United States Military Academy.

- Pat Custer, former Chairman/CEO of Curtis Mathes Corporation and former President of the Donny Osmond Entertainment Corporation. Currently, he is an International Business Advisor specializing on Asia and more specifically on China. Pat has appeared on TV networks CNN, CNNfN, Bloomberg, CBS, and Fox News. He is a modern day Renaissance man and I call him the Six Million Mile Man because he has accumulated at least that many miles from all his travels. He once showed me a 3 Million Mile card from just one airline.

- Dr. Steven Howe, Director of the Center for Space Nuclear Research. A celebrity scientist and fiction writer, published the novella, Wrench and Claw and Honor Bound Honor Born which details the possible development of the first commercial base on the Moon. Steve has also appeared in numerous television programs about space and rocketry. His television credits include '*Living and Working in Space*', PBS and Sci-Fi Channel, '*Mission to Mars*', Ultra Science, the Learning Channel, '*Rocketships*', Discovery Channel, '*Rockets in Space*', Wingspan, and '*Voyage to the Milky Way*', PBS.

- Robert Crandall, former Chairman and CEO of American Airlines and the creator of one of the first frequent flyer programs in the airline industry. Currently, he is the CEO of POGO, a company that will offer personal air travel that is convenient and cost effective via 'very light jets' that can land at smaller airports.

- Gwen Chang, my former roommate in New York City. Her father is now a Senator in Taiwan. He was also the former advisor on Russian policies to U.S. President Ronald Reagan.

- Gloria Blackman, former nanny to my kids and mother to Rolando Blackman, one of only two basketball players in Dallas Mavericks history to have his number retired. Rolando is now the Assistant Coach for the Dallas Mavericks, finalists in the 2006 NBA championship.

- Joe Namath, former football quarterback for the 1969 Super Bowl champion New York Jets. Joe is best known for publicly guaranteeing that the New York Jets would beat the heavily-favored Baltimore Colts in Super Bowl III. Inducted into the Pro Football Hall of Fame in 1985, he also served as an analyst for NBC Sports and ABC's Monday Night Football.

- Roger Staubach, former football quarterback for the 1972 and 1978 Super Bowl champion Dallas Cowboys. Inducted into the Pro Football Hall of Fame in 1985. Awarded the Heisman Trophy in 1963.

- Coach Tom Landry, former coach for the 1972 and 1978 Super Bowl champion Dallas Cowboys. Coached an NFL-record 20 consecutive winning seasons with the Dallas Cowboys. Inducted into the Pro Football Hall of Fame in 1990.

- Ross Perot Jr., Chairman and former CEO of Perot Systems Corporation, and former owner of the Dallas Mavericks. His father, Ross Perot Sr., is co-founder of EDS, a Dallas computer billionaire, philanthropist and independent (Reform Party) candidate for U.S. president in 1992 and 1996.

- Tom McCartin, a former advisor to one of my startup companies, former publisher of the Dallas Times Herald and the Washington Post during the Richard Nixon era. Tom was a great man, always standing up for the little guy.

- Ellen Simonetti, a former roommate, author of Diary of a Dysfunctional Flight Attendant. Ellen is the most talked about ex-Delta Airlines flight attendant. She is the 'Queen of Sky, the Famous Fired Flight Attendant.' Supposedly fired for posting inappropriate pictures in a Delta Airlines uniform on her blog. Her story has been featured in numerous magazines and on radio stations and TV shows. She even received a pair of basketball tickets from Mark Cuban for the Dallas Mavericks game which we attended together.

- David Jackson, one of my college buddies and whistleblower to a corporate corruption case unfolding as this book is being written. David has been working in the investment management business for the last eight years. According to his calculations the wrong-doings that he observed have cost the investors tens, if not hundreds of millions of dollars. No longer with that company, he's currently trying to get his former employer to reimburse the victims of its negligence and fraud for the money that they have lost. In this case, the collision of corporate intransigence and my friend's stick-to-it-ness can only mean that this is more than likely going to end in another headline-screaming scandal. A special investigative committee has been formed, comprising the same legal team members that were involved in the WorldCom and Enron investigations.

- Jeff Brady, anchor for the Dallas ABC affiliate TV station, who covered a story on OxySure, one of NTEC's program companies. Some of the most interesting stories that Jeff has covered in the past include the Super Bowl, the Space Shuttle program, a UN Naval blockade near Haiti, civil violence in Southern Mexico, and the Clinton-Gore Presidential motorcade through Texas during the 2000 election.

- Phil Romano, renowned entrepreneur and restaurateur of a $10 billion food empire which includes Fuddruckers, Romano's Macaroni Grill, Spageddies, Cozymel's, Rudy's Country Store & BBQ, and eatZi's Market & Bakery.

- Kristi Overgaard, former marketing and advertising genius behind the Howard Hughes Corporation, the world's most successful real estate development firm. Howard Hughes was the eccentric billionaire businessman, aviator, movie producer, developer, etc. Based in Las Vegas, Kristi is the founder of 'one11,' a high design firm that specializes in imaging, branding, advertising, and placemaking.

- Hans Streich, a former business partner, creator of the logos for the 7-Eleven chain of convenience stores, Schepps dairy, Golden Apple Teacher Award, and the Marlboro cigarettes packages.

- Sonya Fairbanks, an accomplished artist, widely known for her exquisite and sensual still life pastels and paintings. In 1999, she was admitted into the Pastel Society of America, as well as being featured in American Artist and Southwest Art. Sonya was married to the nephew of Douglas Fairbanks, an actor, screenwriter, director, and producer, who became noted for his roles in movies such as The Mark of Zorro, Three Musketeers, Robin Hood, et al.

- George Takai, best known for his portrayal of Mr. Sulu in the acclaimed television and film series Star Trek. He has more than 30 feature films and hundreds of television guest-starring roles to his credit. He received a star on Hollywood Boulevard's Walk of Fame in 1986, and he placed his signature and hand print in the forecourt of the landmark Grauman's Chinese Theater in Hollywood in 1991. His distinctive voice is featured in many full-length animated features including Mulan and Mulan II, The

Simpsons, Futurama, etc. I have a signed copy of his autobiography titled, To the Stars.

- Bill Cosby, actor, comedian, television producer, activist, creator of the cartoon series Fat Albert and the Cosby Kids, producer and star of The Cosby Show which aired from 1984 to 1992. He was also a spokesman for products like Jell-O Pudding and Coca-Cola.

- Madison and Devin, my daughters and actors on the TV show Barney & Friends. Both were included in a video on fire safety with Barney and currently playing small roles on the Barney & Friends PBS Kids TV. I think they will be famous one day...

It's amazing when I look back to see how far I've reached from the crowded transport airplane flying away from a world of chaos and destruction, to the company of these distinguished people who have left their mark on our society. The list above is just an example of how connected we all are in this web of life.

In our technical society, it is easier than ever to be connected, especially via the internet and various online networking websites, like myspace.com, linkedin.com, blogger.com. I'm directly linked to networks of thousands of people around the world helping each other find jobs and investment opportunities, as well as connecting with like-minded people. In essence, I can say, "*I know a person, who knows a person, that knows a person*," and that's how I get things done.

A word of caution about the use of technology to network. Technically, the world is more connected than ever before. However, social relationships are becoming more and more disconnected. Technology has provided us with more knowledge, freedom, and independence, but it is only a tool to begin developing social skills. To connect on a personal level, there is no replacement for a one on one, face to face interaction.

The art of networking is very simple. Read up on current events so you can engage in small talk with just anyone. Do your homework and be prepared before attending any settings. Be courteous, considerate, and helpful to the people you meet. Introduce yourself and help introduce others. Take good notes and be responsive in following up. If you are an inquisitive person, networking can be almost effortless. Only by asking questions will you find a connection.

There is a growing awareness of connectivity and the collective consciousness is growing exponentially. For me, it's clear that in addition to who you are, it's who you know that takes you places. This network of acquaintances will grow into friendships or business partnerships down the road. You will become the average of those that surround you and they will help you achieve your goals.

Through networking I found my first job and my previous job. This was also how I met my best friend and many real friends ever since. For me, real friends are the ones that give their time and efforts when you need them and they expect nothing in return. These friendships have endured the test of time, some lasting for over 25 years which is rare by today's standards. Many new friendships continue to be made as I travel to expand my knowledge and network.

The world is constantly changing. It is becoming more and more complex with overwhelming choices, so access to good information is vital. By expanding your network, you will have access to information which will give you the ability to make better predictions about how the world works. That's a significant competitive advantage.

However, I'm still learning. There is a saying, "*the more I read, the less I know*." The lesson here is that we are just infants in learning how to link our body and mind to the rest of the world. As we expand our network, the world will become more apparent. Life is a stage for us to unfold our performances and everyone has a story to tell.

'If you have extra income, spend it on experiences instead of more stuff.' The extra income is best spent on things that will let you grow as an individual like networking, education, recreation, social activities, and travel. A good portion of my income is spent on traveling and networking. As I travel connections are made, my network continues to expand, and the story of the world is becoming more complete.

St. Augustine, the philosopher, once said, "*The world is a book, and those who don't travel, only read one page*." I intend to finish the entire book.

Photo 1, Left: My Mom and Dad in Vietnam, the early years.

Photo 2, Right: Mom and Dad at their wedding.

Photo 3, Left: I'm on a Vespa scooter.

Photo 4, Right: With my Mom.

Photo 5, Left: My Mom and some of my siblings. I'm on the wooden horse.

Photo 6, Bottom: Family photo with us kids. I'm in the front on the right.

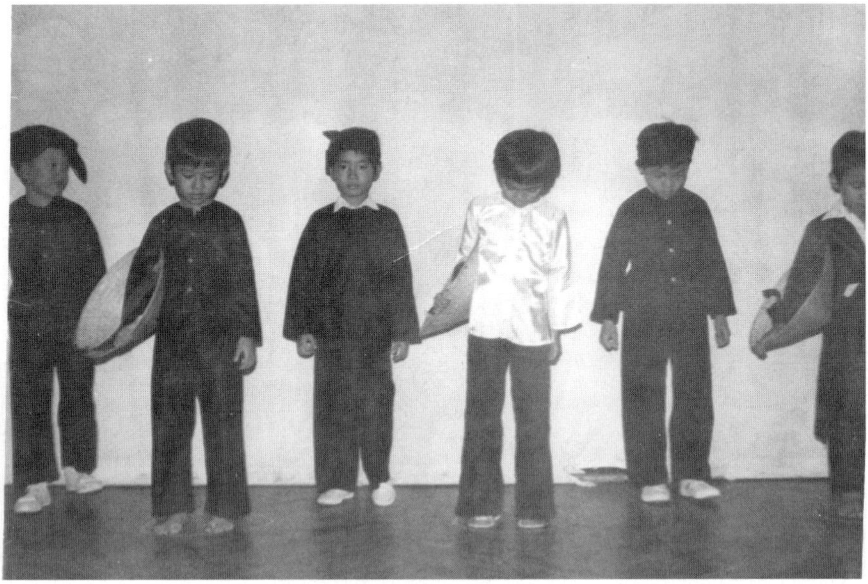

Photo 7, Top: I'm in white bowing to the audience at a theater performance.

Photo 8, Bottom: In the marching band. I'm at the front playing the clarinet.

Photo 9, Left: I'm in my Little League baseball uniform.

Photo 10, Right: My brother and I after winning a tennis tournament. I'm on the right, holding two trophies.

Photo 11, Top: Receiving a merit badge in Boy Scouts. I'm in the middle.

Photo 12, Bottom: As an altar boy leading a Catholic mass.

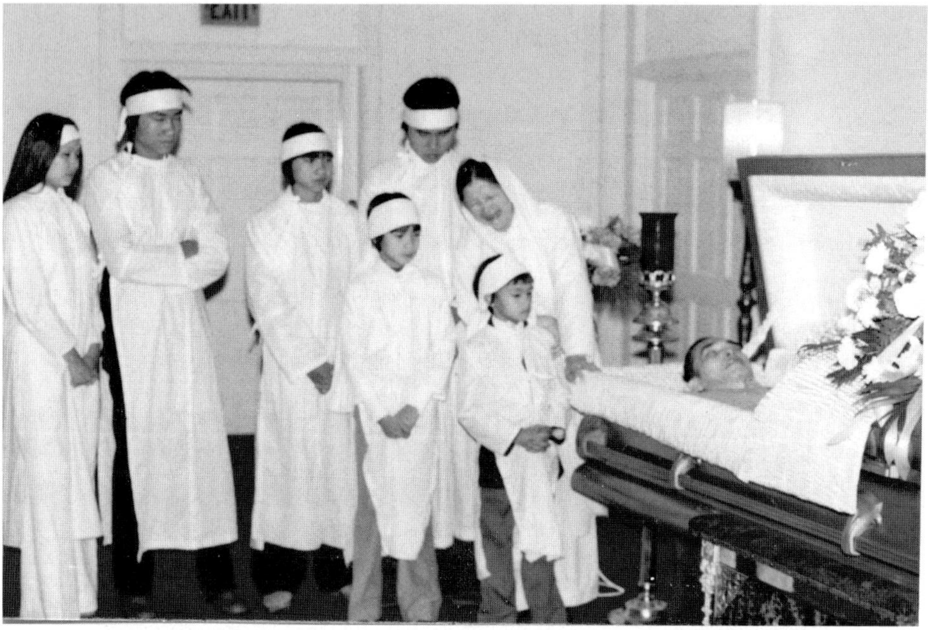

Photo 13, Top: My dad's funeral. I'm third from the left. The Vietnamese tradition is to wear white at a funeral.

Photo 14, Left: Waiting to receive my graduate diploma from The University of Texas.

Photo 15, Bottom: Hang gliding off the coast of Rio, Brazil.

Photo 16, Top: With a friend in Tiananmen Square in Beijing, China.

Photo 17, Bottom: My days as a fencer after winning the Texas Team Championship in Kendo. We won a trophy and a case of beer. I'm on the far left.

Photo 18, Top: My days as a swordsman practicing Iaido.

Photo 19, Bottom: At a martial arts demonstration. I'm on the left.

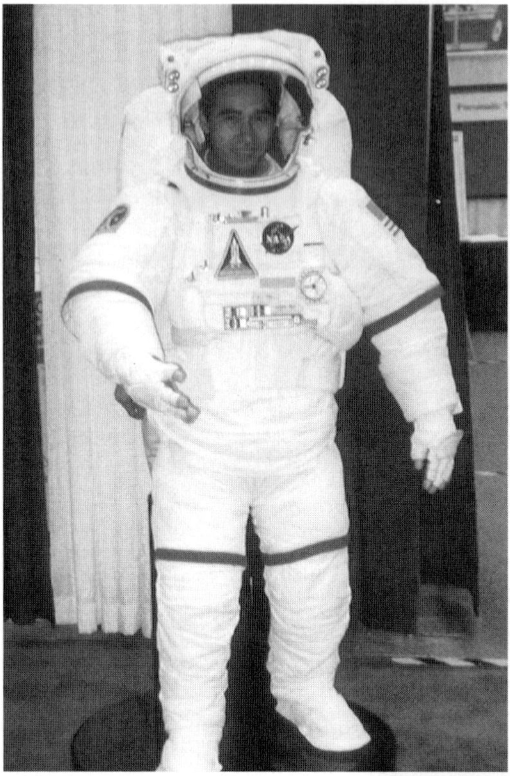

Photo 20, Left: Playing around in a space suit at the NASA Johnson Space Center.

Photo 21, Right: With Ellen Simonetti, author of 'Diary of a Dysfunctional Flight Attendant.' She is the 'Queen of Sky, the Famous Fired Flight Attendant.'

Photo 22, Top: I'm with Joe Namath, the legendary football quarterback and Hall of Famer.

Photo 23, Bottom: My group of student interns with Phil Pozderac, former football lineman for the Dallas Cowboys. I'm on the far left.

Photo 24, Top: Presenting the MEDTEC Achievement Award to Julian Ross, founder of OxySure Systems, Inc.

Photo 25, Bottom: With friends, Minister Liang (middle) and his deputies from China. I'm second from the left.

Photo 26, Top: With friends and Dr. Steven Howe (far left), a celebrity scientist and Director of the Center for Space Nuclear Research. I'm in the middle.

Photo 27, Right: With my business partner Larry Calton, Executive Director of the North Texas Enterprise Center for Medical Technology.

The Business of Sex, Love, and Marriage

"*What does love have to do with it?*" If anyone really knows what sex, love, and marriage are all about, please raise your hand because you deserve a lifetime achievement award for solving one of the greatest mysteries in the Universe. There are so many interpretations of sex, love, and marriage, and it is such an illogical topic. I had to take some time out while writing this book to rummage around my memories to reassess what it felt like to be in love and to be married. The following stories reveal my personal experience with sex, love, and marriage from a perspective that will probably raise a few eyebrows.

Up until my college years I did not have much of a social life. I couldn't afford to go out, so I didn't begin dating until I was in college. As it turns out, I fell in love with the first girl that showed interest in me. Her name was Jody. I noticed her in one of my classes and we later met at a student dance. Jody was from South Korea. She immigrated to the U.S. when her family was exiled after the assassination of South Korea's President Park Chung Hee in 1979.

Jody and I had a very intense love-hate relationship that lasted about three years. Since every emotion we experienced together was a first for both of us, at the end we were emotional wrecks. Jody was naturally gifted as an artist, a bit neurotic, but a very caring person. We both knew we were in love. We couldn't wait to see each other everyday and our stomachs were constantly filled with butterflies. It was very passionate while it lasted. But we were too young and too inexperienced to know what was happening.

In addition, she had tremendous pressures from her Korean friends ridiculing her for dating a non-Korean which did not help the situation. As far as our first sexual experience, we were both virgins when we met, so the first time was very awkward. It was brief, uneventful, and unforgettable. We went our separate ways when I left for my jobs in Europe and she went back to South Korea a few years later after her graduation.

It took me a few years before I could bring myself to date again. That was when I lived in New York City. My best friend Kyle was in town and he called a friend from college whom we both knew. We all met for dinner one night. Her name was Janet. I had no idea we were living in the same city. We ended up dating. The next thing I knew I'm at a courthouse getting married. It was somewhat of a lackluster wedding. The best man and witness to the event was some guy we grabbed from the courthouse lobby.

Let me explain how this happened. Janet came to the U.S. on a student visa. To be able to stay and work in the U.S., she needed to get a work visa from an employer who was willing to sponsor her, or she needed to be married to a U.S. citizen. Since we were dating anyway, I agreed to marry her and we stayed together until she was able to apply for a permanent residency status. Then it was no longer necessary for us to be married. Three years later, we went our separate ways and continued to remain friends. The relationship was lukewarm at best and the years went by quickly as we were both very busy with our own careers. In essence, my first marriage was a business arrangement.

Approaching 30! At this point in my life, I was ready to settle down and to start a family. That was when I met Brandy. We met at a night club and found out that we worked for the same company. The chemistry was there and we immediately began dating the next evening. We were inseparable. I didn't waste any time. I proposed to Brandy at the zoo a few months later. Within a year, we got married in Las Vegas at the Excalibur Hotel by Merlin the Wizard. Brandy came from a humble background. She was raised on a dairy farm in Oklahoma. She was a typical farm girl with blonde hair, blue eyes, and she has a great personality.

A year after we were married, we had our first child Madison. A year after that we had our second child Devin. The two days when our kids were born were the happiest days in my life. There is something surreal about holding a newborn in your arms and knowing you had something to do with the process. At that point in my life everything was great. I felt like I had attained the American Dream. I was now a father and a husband. I had a great career, a cozy home, nice cars, and good friends. What else can you get out of life?!

Then one night I had an epiphany of a dream. I will write more about the dream later in the chapter '*The Search for God and Spirituality.*' That dream changed my perception of reality and my priorities in life.

Overnight, my senses went into overdrive and I awoke with a brand new perspective on life. I began to follow my intuition in search for the meaning of my dream. I began to gravitate towards people who were more self-aware and who were reaching beyond the realm of everyday existence. As a result, we drifted apart and our marriage began to disintegrate.

Needless to say, Brandy and everyone around me thought I was insane. So I agreed to counseling. We met with a psychologist a few times and he was puzzled. At first, he did his usual probe to try to identify the root of the problem. But the more he probed, I think, the more confused he became. We seem to have had the perfect marriage. There was no drug problem, no alcohol problem, no financial problem, no infidelity problem, and we never had any real disagreements.

Then came the professional analysis. I was diagnosed with bipolar disorder. This was a shocker for me and my friends. I never took the diagnosis seriously and never took any medicine or sought any more therapy. All I needed was space and the freedom to begin my quest, so I took it.

Brandy filed for divorce soon afterwards. She was confused and did what needed to be done in order to secure a comfortable lifestyle for herself and the kids. She was emotionally distraught and began seeking legal help at a most vulnerable time. The attorney fees began to mount. I objected at first but I knew at the time that emotions would overrule any logic. I let it be and did not seek any legal support to counteract. When the dust settled, I lost everything. I was basically homeless and penniless. We did sit down a year later by ourselves, with no attorney, and resettled everything to what was fair for both sides. The interesting part about this experience is that we kept it quiet among my friends and most of them never knew we were divorced. We were together for about six years. We continue to be friends and we enjoy having a great time raising our children.

Life after the divorce was not much fun as I was trying to gather the pieces to start over. Being genetically programmed to find a mate, I was determined to find a new love. As my life began to take shape again, I submerged into reading relationship books to learn how to date again. I must have read over 20 books on relationships, from '1001 Ways to be Romantic', to 'Relationship Rescue', to 'Men are from Mars, Women are from Venus.' In addition, I scoured the internet for countless websites trying to unlock the mystery behind sex, love, and marriage. This time around, I wanted to be more prepared. With my research, I was hoping to find a new perspective into how the dating game is played.

While sorting through the noise, it dawned on me that I had been a victim of the fairy tales of Prince Charming and the Princess Bride. Call me naïve but only now did I realize that sex, love, and marriage are basically business arrangements. Like all kids growing up, I loved fairy tales, especially those where the prince gets to marry the princess. Fairy tales are great at teaching us ethics and morals, but I believe they provide a false sense of hope and an illusion about love and marriage. We have all been inundated with love fairy tales growing up but when reality hits, the true meaning of marriage surfaces with its original intentions.

From my research, I've found that in most ancient societies, the institution of marriage was meant to secure an environment for the perpetuation of the species, to handle the granting of properties, and to protect the bloodlines. The couples involved did not have much say about the decision. Most did not marry because they were in love but rather did it for 'economic reasons'. Some marriages were by proxy. Some involved a dowry where a bride's family gave money or presents to the groom or his family. Some required a bride price where the groom or his family gave money or a present to the bride's family.

Over time, marriage has been romanticized. It has become a bond between two people that involves responsibility, legalities, commitment, and challenge, but the underlying economic reasons have not changed. Today, not only is marriage considered as a source of wealth, it also provides for other needs such as sexual satisfaction, emotional bonding, social prestige, and social benefits.

So here I was, 36 years old, in a new millennium, armed with my newfound wisdom. I was ready to jump back into the dating game where all is fair in love and war, a competition that is not for the faint of heart. The landscape has changed dramatically since I dated. Now there are many ways to connect from speed dating and blind dates, to online dating, to matchmaking gurus, to the bar and club scenes. I was reluctant at first but I began building some confidence and gave each method a try.

The dating process was very tedious. I felt like a tape recorder being rewound every time I met a new woman. But it was an interesting experiment. I kept notes on most women that I had a conversation with and recorded some of their wildest comments. Most of the time, these women had a few drinks and were nervous themselves, so they didn't really know what they were saying or even remembered what had transpired.

TEN QUOTES FROM WOMEN I'VE JUST MET:

"What do you drive? Do you own a home? When are we going to Mexico?"

"You're in medical? Could you feel my breasts to see if I need implants?"

"This is my husband, we're swingers, would you like to join us?"

"I think I'm drunk, here are my keys, can you take me home?"

"My rate is $1,000 an hour, but it's negotiable"

"When is your birthday? Mine is 1-23-69"

"I often see ghosts and aliens hiding in my room"

"I have never been with anyone other than white people"

"I'm insulted that you think I'm after your money." A few days later, "Exactly, how much money do you have?"

"I'm a newlywed, so I don't want you to waste your time." Three hours later, "We're both going to hell."

After a few dates, I quickly recognized why certain women have such difficulty finding a healthy relationship. Many are unprepared for real life. Many are emotionally challenged, living with regrets, fear, and anger. Some continue to portray themselves as victims of society. Others don't know who they are or what they want and they expect somebody to come and fill the void in their lives and souls.

Below is a list of some women that I've encountered in various settings with personalities that are worth mentioning.

The Unemployed

Sheri was a well educated woman with a Ph.D. degree but she was unemployed when we first met for dinner. At the outset, she began complaining about how hard it is for a woman to find a job in this town. Without thinking I said, "*Anyone can find a job if they really wanted a job.*" She didn't take that too well and got up and left. This date lasted less than 15 minutes.

The Schizophrenic

Tina was a very nice woman afflicted with some form of neurological disorder that makes her see images of ghosts and aliens at a moment's notice. It was very confusing having a conversation with her while she kept drifting into other dimensions.

The Furious

Alice was a woman who didn't handle rejection well. At the end of dinner one evening, I told her that we're not compatible. She became furious, and kicked over the dining table as we were leaving the restaurant, and ran off.

The Alcoholic

Katy was voted as one of the most beautiful girls in her high school and college. She acknowledged that she did not know how beautiful she was when growing up. She often self-medicated with alcohol, living with regrets, and looking for love in all the wrong places. She was artistically gifted and spiritually connected but she was often drunk. When we first met at a club, she gave me the keys to her car and apartment, and asked to be taken home. Later, I found out that she was previously arrested for driving under the influence but didn't remember anything that happened.

The Stalker

Connie was on the rebound when we met. We had a great evening out. We ran into a friend of hers. She later shared that her ex-husband kicked down her friend's door when he thought they were dating. The next morning, I got a knock on my door from some guy in a red pickup truck. I didn't answer the door and never went out with her again. Later, I found out that she stalked her ex-husband one morning at 5:00 a.m. and repossessed his truck.

The Dancer

Teresa was a single mother. She was a real estate agent by day and topless dancer by night which she revealed to me after a few cups of coffee. When we first met for coffee, she asked if I would like to come and watch her dance. Between home schooling her daughter and working two jobs at odd hours, she didn't have much of a social life and often lived in seclusion. She desperately wanted a relationship but couldn't seem to find the time.

The Recently Divorced

Anna broke all the rules on what not to talk about on a first date. She brought up the various topics of marriage, divorce, religion, spirituality, politics, children, exes, sex, job, money, etc. There was not much that didn't come up. Then she broke down crying about how lost she felt. In all, I think she just needed an outlet for her feelings after a divorce, so that she could start a new life.

The Newlywed

Amanda was a newlywed with many regrets. Her biological clock was ticking. She got married for the wrong reason and had regretted her decision ever since. She was on a business trip when we met at a lounge. Her first comment was "I'm a newlywed, so I don't want you to waste your time." Three hours later, she said, "We're both going to hell."

Woman on the Verge

Cathy was a woman on the verge of a nervous breakdown. After several dates, I realized that she was not well. She stressed out easily from work and school, and she often drifted into depression. Then one day, she snapped and had a nervous breakdown. She was found by the police running around the streets, blocking traffic, to warn people about the aliens and terrorists coming to kill them. She was taken to a mental hospital and kept there for six months. I later found out that her family had a history of mental illness. That experience was an eye opener for me on how mental illness is diagnosed and treated.

The Phobic

Leslie was one of the most gifted artists and neurotic women that I have ever known. At first glance, she was well spoken with a great personality and as nice as could be. She seemed to be in total control of her life. A few weeks passed and I began to notice some unusual behavior. Without notice, she would exhibit various phobias such as a fear of being touched, a fear of certain foods, or a fear of people walking beside her, myself included. However, these fears came and went. Sometimes certain noises, words, or images would bring about the strangest reaction and profanity would come out of nowhere as she became overly suspicious.

As I learned more about her background, it became evident that she was struggling with multiple personalities. This was her way of coping with her anxiety. She also later admitted to being a recovering alcoholic who used alcohol to self-medicate in order to suppress her unhappy childhood memories and past relationships, which may have contributed to her personification of the victim syndrome. When we last spoke, she was searching for meanings and sorting out her identities to begin a new life.

Just so that there is no misunderstanding, I want to point out that the above personalities reflect various stages in one's life and are relevant only to my own experience. They are not a true representation of the majority of women out there. I'm certain there are many wonderful women who are emotionally stable and well-prepared for a fulfilling relationship.

Overall, the dating game in today's environment has changed considerably from when I dated originally. It is a lot more complex than I remember. Everyone seems to be in a rush and life is more demanding than ever. Age and looks are still very important for first impressions and it is very difficult to recover if the initial chemistry is not there. Also, due to the increasing use of cosmetic surgery, it's becoming more and more difficult to tell someone's age.

There is a stereotype that if a woman is not married or in a relationship by the time she is 30, she is considered excessively difficult. As for a man, if he is not involved by the time he is 35, he is considered gay. If you're divorced with kids, it is assumed that there is something wrong with you. The times have also changed as to who is the initiator and who pays. As more women are gaining financial independence, they often tend to be the aggressor and the instigator for the initial date.

Furthermore, whether people are subconsciously aware of it or not, the mind game is still the same. Men continue to flaunt their wealth and women continue to flaunt their beauty to attract attention. Then, the seduction process begins to see who gains control of the heart, mind, and the pocketbook. For me, it was obvious that underneath the facade, most men are out looking for sex while most women are in search of comfort and security in this game of love and entrapment.

What makes it even more difficult to date in the city of Dallas is the fact that there is a great pressure to keep up with the Joneses. A lot of people here fall into the material trap and live well beyond their means. They are sometimes referred to as the $30,000 millionaires, faking what they don't have, living from paycheck to paycheck.

For now, I'm just taking a break and enjoying the scenery. Interestingly, my daughters wrote a list for me of criteria and tests for selecting my next girlfriend and which I have attached in the following pages.

What they should look like

1. Eyes: Blue, Brown, or Torquase. No glasses.
2. Nose: small.
3. Hair: Long, brown, blond
4. Size: Shorter than Dad
5. body: Skinny. light brown skin or white skin. Nice odor. No pimples
6. Ears: Someone with earings.
7. Fingers: crystal clear or dark pollish.
8. Shoes: high hells Black, brown, white or gold.
9. Shirt: Sleevles or short short sleeves. Tanktops

girlfriends
tests

1 Choose 1 dog out of 4 dogs.
1 Burp test
2 baking test, Bake something with
2 a small amount of food.
3 Snoring test:
3
4 Walking the dog test.

5 Hairstyle on yourself.

6 Talent test: Show your talent, Splits, cartwheel.
7 Sport test: Show ~~the~~ your sport in action
8 style test. Show your style
9 Cleaning test: Clean our messes.

10 essay: on dad,
11 attatoode; We act up what do you do.
12 swimming test
13 Art test; Draw a dog or dad
14 Music test, Sing or use an instrument
15 Favorite color.
~~16~~

I'm often asked if I have given up on dating. Weary of the mind games being played and tired of walking on eggshells to avoid emotional landmines, I decided to become a benchwarmer. I was having too much fun enjoying the single life to waste my time in dating games. I stayed on the sidelines to observe the human animal in its natural environment. This is where I collected even more interesting stories. No matter how many books you've read, it's impossible to understand the full breadth of the words until you are exposed to those experiences in person. I was about to get a complete education in human sexuality.

Being a travel bug, both for pleasure and for business, I get to meet a lot of interesting people and they are more than eager to tell their life stories. They all want to be heard and be connected. They tend to be more adventurous and less guarded when on vacation, while doing things that they may not otherwise do when at home. From their stories and connections, I was exposed to some of the most unusual encounters and exotic scenes. I began taking notes to further understand the human mating ritual and its evolution into modern day businesses. Below are a few venues and facts that I stumbled upon in the process that are worth revealing about the business of sex, love, and marriage.

The Online Matchmaker

The Internet provides the most popular modern-day venue for two individuals to get connected; and, matchmaking is one of the main reasons for the proliferation of the Internet. From aol.com, myspace.com, eharmony.com, to match.com, more and more people are finding sex, love, and marriage online.

Online matchmakers are selling the dream and the unlimited possibility of being who you want to be, hidden behind the anonymous computer screen. The choices are almost infinite but here lies the trouble. You may find the one little thing you don't like about the 'match' and move on. It sometimes is too easy. Lured by the promise and availability of millions of online singles, it is easy to forget that people do not come in black and white, and you can not have your custom-made dream partner ordered and delivered on the Internet.

Online dating is also an arena for liars, criminals, and married people. Often, online profiles are not a true representation of the person. Most people perceive themselves much differently than from other's perception of them. Just as in real life, more choices bring more responsibilities.

Technology is here to help. From an inside source, I was given a glimpse into how data is gathered, how algorithms are developed, and how this 'online dating deal' works. You can restrict your search criteria down to any level you want. You can be assured that you will be matched only with people who will find you attractive. Sometimes you learn more about a person from their online profile and a few chat sessions or emails than they will be willing to share in a few months of dating. The database of millions of singles is there to provide you with instant results for your search. Almost too good to be true! We seem to forget that at some point, regardless of when and how it started, we have to take it to the real world. And there, we are on our own.

But the dream is selling. Everyone is lured to the exciting fantasy of changing their life overnight, of 'hitting the jackpot' and walking out as a winner. But just like in the casino, the online matchmaker knows that the odds are against the players. The only real winner is 'the house,' unless you know some secret magic to turn the odds around.

Online matchmaking is a solid business machine with many returning customers, cashing in on the innermost human desire to feel close and connected to each other. No wonder it's one of the fastest growing Internet businesses, especially when the New Year's resolutions kick in, or it's time to face yet another lonely Valentine's day.

The Offshore Matchmaker

The business of sex, love, and marriage is also taken offshore. Just like any business, when it is no longer feasible to get the job done at home, you look to outsource abroad. With all the different ways of getting connected in America, people are paying top dollars to go abroad to look for sex, and, if they are lucky, they will find love and marriage.

Designed mostly to serve men, there are organized networks for mail-ordered mates running from Europe to Latin America, to Asia, targeting mostly Third World countries. Events and trips called 'romance tours' are organized on a monthly basis to match the fortunate seekers with the available brides who are willing to offer their bodies and hearts in exchange for a hope of escaping poverty.

I have always been wondering how it worked. Then one day I met a few couples who went through the process. They were happy with the results, as both parties got what they needed. In some Third World countries, the matchmaking business is the main source of revenue for its citizens.

The Adult Entertainment Industry

The oldest industry intertwined with the oldest profession in the history of the world. If it were not for sex, history would not exist.

Being involved in various business ventures and having to entertain clients, I can't help but be associated with some of the most beautiful women in this industry. Over the years, I became very familiar with the 'business' and how much money can be made. The topless clubs make most of their money on liquor sales. The dancers that I've met can make up to $150k per year, and the average prostitute can make as much as $200k per year, tax free. It was also interesting to find out that to dance in a club, a fee must be paid every night by the girls and anything over that fee, the girls get to keep as profit.

However, this is a short-lived career laced with drugs and alcohol, which often lead to violence and accidents. That was evident one rainy night when my friend and I were rear-ended by a drunk driver. The driver happened to be a woman who just liquored herself to gain the nerve to start her new job as a topless dancer. She totally wrecked her car and was in no condition to drive, so we drove her home. We were led on an hour long drive to some trailer home and later were accused by her friends of drugging her. They threatened to call the police to have us arrested. We left the scene and laughed about it. We could have had her arrested for drunk driving. Sometimes being a Good Samaritan can backfire.

The Bed Buddy System

The bed buddy is simply a partner for casual sex. This is the most prevailing and sustainable form of intimate relationships these days. It's easy and convenient. No hopes and no promises. Everything is at face value. Many people are doing it but nobody wants to admit that they have done it or find it appealing. The single scene is flooded with hormones running rampant. At midnight in any given bar or club, there is no shortage of people trying to hook-up for the night. I've been on trips with friends where after a night of drinking most people have no problem with exposing themselves. Most can't even remember who they slept with the night before. In several instances, we would run into the same woman the next day and she would be clueless about who we were.

One night out, there was this one outrageous scene when a woman showed up at a bar in a five-star hotel wearing no pants. At first glance, it looked like she had a very short jacket on. As she approached the bar and bent over to order a drink, everything was exposed. The security guard had to come over to escort her back to her room. Apparently, a few hours before, she was having dinner with a friend and had a bit too much to drink. They went back to the room for some action but she wasn't done drinking. She came back downstairs for another drink and forgot to put her pants back on.

Being single can be lonely at times, especially in today's environment where everyone seems to be caught in a rat race with no time for a real relationship. To compensate for this, a bed buddy system in which the sex is casual, convenient, and commitment-free has become a trend. I was even approached by a friend with the idea about a new website called 'friend buddy.' I did my own research, since this is a delicate and risky business. The result was that some people denounced the idea as hedonistic, morally corrupt, and they believed, contained the potential for emotional disaster. On the other side, for people who have established a successful bed buddy system where there is no-strings-attached sex, it's a highly recommended arrangement as a hormonal cure-all and a means to fulfill sexual desires and boost personal egos.

However, under the cover of the bed buddy system, and, I suspect for the long haul, everyone will still be on the lookout for their soulmate.

The Swingers' Club

The swingers' club is an alternative sexual playground for couples, mainly heterosexual. I was first introduced to this lifestyle by Tara, a woman I met at a local hangout known to attract "gold diggers," that is people looking to trap wealthy individuals. Interestingly, Tara became one of my business investors afterwards. "The economic is simple," said Tara, "adding that by the time you take a woman out for dinner, theater, drinks, and dancing, you would already have spent over $300 and there is no guarantee that you'll get lucky that night. For $75, you can spend the entire evening at a swingers' club and meet as many women as you can handle." Well, I couldn't argue with that logic, so she took me and my friends to the club for a tour.

When we arrived, the place was very nice and clean, seemingly catered to the well-to-do. We were all very eager and excited to see more. To gain access, men are required to be accompanied by a woman, whereas single women are generally welcomed. It is a club like any other upscale clubs with the exception that half the women are walking around in their birthday suits, or dressed up for the theme of the evening. The most memorable sight from this experience was a couple wearing nothing but bells tied to their arms, legs, and necks. So every time they 'had some fun,' we could hear them jingling.

In this environment, the women are often the instigators, if there is any interest in you or your partner. I'm sure this lifestyle sounds very interesting and intriguing to a lot of people out there. Keep in mind that the swinging lifestyle should not be used as a means for replacing a failing sexual relationship but rather as a means for enhancing your sex-life together. I have met a few couples there and we became friends, only to hear later that they were no longer together. In this setting, it is quite common for jealousy to arise due to insecurity. If your relationship is not a sturdy one, then jealousy, anger, betrayal, and every other irrational emotion will take over, quickly destroying what was left of your relationship.

We had a great time and to date, the club is one of the places I would recommend for anyone looking for a new and unforgettable experience. One thing I learned from this experience is that monogamy is a choice or a lifestyle. It is definitely not natural for the human animal.

The Wonder Drugs

Viagra is a drug initially developed for a heart condition but was found to give some 'heads-up' to men. Thus, a billion-dollar market for erectile dysfunction (ED) drugs was instantly created and it grew. Today, there are over a dozen ED drugs on the market but along with the solutions they bring, come the side effects. The increased use of Viagra and related drugs has been determined to contribute to increased sexual activity which in turn has caused increasing rate of sexually transmitted diseases.

Another interesting fact I received from one of our medical advisors is that women in their 50's and 60's are coming in droves to clinics wanting a surgical procedure done to have a functional vagina again. As more and more of their partners are using ED drugs, they too want a treatment to enhance their sex lives. According to research done by the University of Chicago, some 43 percent of women suffer from sexual dysfunction compared to 31 percent of men. The difference between arousal for men and women is that for men it is a physical need rather than an emotional issue. Men need a place for having sex, whereas women need a purpose.

But rest assured, there is a Viagra for women coming in the form of an inhaler or patches to stimulate the brain. It is currently in pre-clinical development and showing promising results. This will create another billion-dollar market for this business of sex.

These are just some of the stories that I can share, but I don't think they say anything that is unique to me. The mystery between men and women is never-ending. The simplest way for me to summarize why men and women are polar opposites is to attach an illustration I received in an email. Men and women are just wired differently!

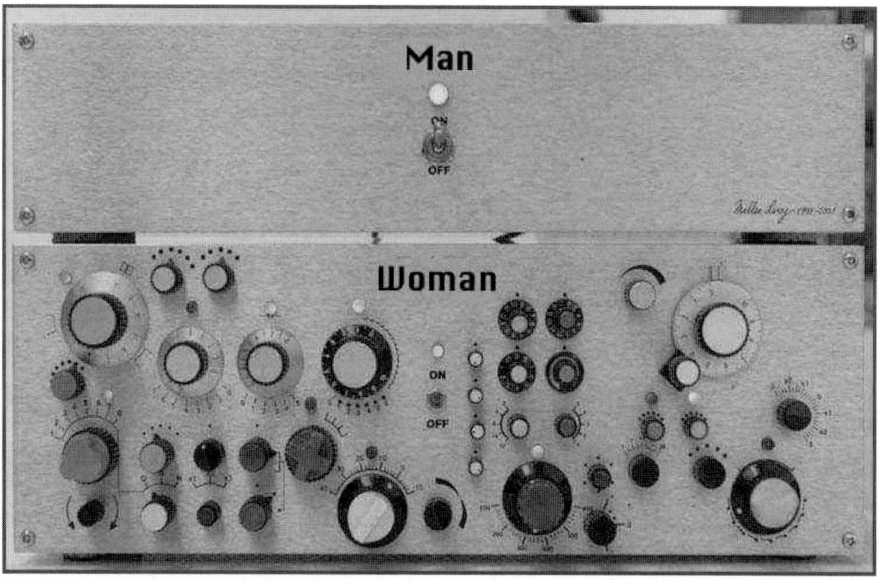

In addition, the mystery of the sexes varies from culture to culture. What is considered desirable in one society can be considered as repulsive in another society. Beauty is truly in the eyes of the beholder!

My suggestion to anyone getting ready to jump back into the dating game is to learn the rules and get some pre-dating counseling, just as you would seek pre-marital counseling before getting married. Acquire as much advice as you can from those who have been there and done that. Let go of the emotional baggage and learn to love yourself first before getting back into the game. Instead of playing all the mind games, just be yourself and you'll find your soulmate in the most unlikely place and when you least expect it.

With the Internet today, finding your mate is not a problem, keeping your mate is. Don't rush into falling in love, because love takes time to build for it to last.

Many people believe love is a spontaneous feeling that magically comes when you meet the right person. The chemistry kicks in and this sensation leads to tremendous hopes and expectations. Love is intoxicating, a chemical imbalance of the brain, an emotional disease to which we are all susceptible. Sometimes these emotions become unstable, leading to disturbing acts of jealousy, hatred, and revenge. No wonder there is so much heartache and disappointment in falling in love.

Love is blind, an irresistible state where emotions suppress rational judgment. In this mode, we tend to overlook the need to assess a person's character and personality. Before leaping into a relationship, take a compatibility test to see if your needs and wants match up. If you are one of the fortunate to have contracted love, cherish it closely, for tomorrow it can spontaneously disappear.

Love is not a necessary ingredient for the marriage lifestyle. If you decide to get married, be sure to obtain a pre-nuptial agreement, because marriage is a business partnership. This partnership is made legal by a verbal contract wrapped in invisible print and hefty termination penalties. In the business of sex, love, and marriage, there are many predators and victims, as both men and women exploit each other. The reality of these partnerships is that they are difficult, draining, and often end in failure.

The main reason why most relationships fail is that we tend to over commit and under deliver, with the illusion that no more efforts are required once a commitment has been established. To build a satisfying relationship, enter the partnership with open eyes and mind. Clarify the skills and contributions that you are bringing to the partnership. Additionally, set realistic expectations for you and your partner to meet, and have them renewed or renegotiated every year.

Sex, love, and marriage are just one facet of life. The sooner you learn to acknowledge the truth behind sex, love, and marriage, the simpler and happier your life will be. Only then will you be ready to journey to the next stage of living. The dilemma here is to find a balance between sex, love, and marriage without sacrificing your identity.

The freedom to fully express yourself in this journey of life should never be compromised. If you can't be yourself, how will you ever be able to discover your destiny?

The Search for God and Spirituality

> ***"When we talk to God, it's called a prayer, but when God talks back, it's called paranoia?"***
>
> -- Anonymous --

I was born a Catholic and educated in a very strict, uniformed Catholic school with the standard corporal punishments. My family was very religious and like most Catholics, we attended mass twice a week, along with all the rituals of baptisms, communions, nightly prayers, etc. I was even an altar boy for 5 years. When I was 20 years old, during my European job experience in Belgium and Italy, I became acquainted with the history of religion, especially the history of the Catholic Church. I often visited the extravagant Vatican in Rome. I quickly realized what religion is all about. To put it simply, organized religion is about wealth, power, and the control of the masses.

From that moment on, I became dismayed with organized religion, especially with how much wealth the Church controlled, not to mention the lavish lifestyle of those in charge preaching to so many suffering in poverty. It is a travesty how these leaders have portrayed God, making a mockery of the image of God to mask their own fear. God needs neither symbol, nor explanation. For me, finding God is basically a matter of individual faith.

I guess you can say that my search for God began early on but it was often interrupted by the American Dream. I was too busy succeeding in the business world, sustaining a nice home, car, family, and keeping up with the Jones. There seemed to be no end as I was sinking deeper and deeper into the rat race. Then all of the sudden, one night I had a dream. It was no ordinary dream. It was more of a revelation, an epiphany. Suddenly, my mind was granted access to information I never knew existed. All my senses have been heightened ever since. I began keeping a dream log and I was even able to control my own dreams.

These dreams were so powerful and vivid that subconsciously, and almost overnight by osmosis, I wrote a paper on the meaning of existence. I had no idea what I just wrote. It felt like I was channeled by someone or something. At the same time, I became a sponge for information and my journey to awareness began. I read somewhere once that in order to find yourself, you have to lose yourself, and did I ever!

For the next few years, I was borderline insane and lost everything close to me. Nothing was more important at the time than chasing my intuition to understand what I wrote. I relinquished my job, house, car, friends and family, wife and kids, and all my life savings. I even considered becoming a monk. Everyone around me thought that I was insane and needed immediate psychological help.

After many months of research, pondering, and wandering, I ended up in Los Alamos, NM, the birthplace of the atomic bomb. While I was working there, during a retreat in the nearby mountains, it dawned on me that the answer lies within myself. The answer was already presented in what I wrote a few years back. I began interpreting my own writings of what it means to exist in a little paper called 'A Theory of Everything.' To this day, I still wonder how I was able to write the paragraphs below with such big words in almost one swoop.

Introduction

Since the beginning of human awareness, the ever-elusive question has always been, 'What is the meaning of life? What is the origin and destination of life? What is the definition of life?'

Life can be defined as any form of a sentient being of energy or matter, which demonstrates a level of consciousness or awareness.

To locate the origin and destination of life in the Universe is to locate the origin and destination of the Universe itself. Life is trapped in an infinite loop of light, space, time, energy, and matter. Therefore, the origin and destination of life is one and the same thing in this infinite loop.

The purpose of formalizing this theory of everything is to bring about a sense of logic behind the meaning of existence for all lifeforms, including their creator. Logically, for anything to exist there must have been a creator, in which the creator itself is a sentient being. It would be rational to acknowledge that a sentient being existed at a given point in time. Over time, the sentient being evolved into various lifeforms, one of which is human beings. The human form, like any other, is a symbiosis of multiple sentient beings, each with its own consciousness. The sum or combination of all individual consciousness gave rise to a unique consciousness that is continuously evolving in the search for the meaning of life.

Thus, the creator of life is also bound by this theory of everything. It states that the meaning of existence for all life revolves around one or all of the following three stages.

The Three Stages

The first stage is to Achieve Happiness, which is a mental state that must be cultivated in order to avoid self-destruction.

The second stage is the Race to Immortality, which is an eternal state of being designed to be seductive, deceptive, and fatally competitive in the process of creating a lifeform capable of enduring all forces of destruction.

The third stage is the Quest for Divine Wisdom, which is an ambivalent state that entails the continuous search for the knowledge of everything, beyond contradicting beliefs, beyond the endless cycle, and beyond infinity.

The paths to Happiness and Immortality are deeply intertwined. They are conceptually a mirage created by a civilization's lifestyles and cultures. However, it is a necessary delusion in providing the foundation to the quest for Divine Wisdom.

The answer is there, waiting to be extrapolated, in which the process, time is irrelevant.

Happiness

"The first stage is to Achieve Happiness, which is a mental state that must be cultivated in order to avoid self-destruction."

Happiness is relative and highly subjective. For some, happiness is a matter of rational fulfillment with one's actions and character. For others, happiness is a state of non-contradictory joy that proceeds from the achievement of one's values. And for many, happiness is the illusionary and temporary satisfaction of the senses. The traditional definition of happiness has been mainly concerned with the attainability and the sustainability of happiness.

As described in the introduction, a lifeform is a symbiosis of multiple sentient beings, each with its own consciousness. On the cellular or molecular level, each cell and molecule in a lifeform is an individual sentient being. The sum or combination of that consciousness gave rise to a unique consciousness. Any attachment to or detachment from a lifeform, whether mentally or physically, initiates a process that is ever evolving in defining and re-defining the consciousness of that lifeform. In other words, consciousness is a physical state of mind. As the mind ages, so does consciousness. This mind-body connection allows the attached lifeforms to exist as one unique consciousness.

The unique consciousness is in a constant struggle to retain cohesion. It must be collectively cultivated through discipline and meditation, in order to decipher conflicting messages circumventing from the individual consciousness and the surrounding environment. Happiness is governed by the state of consciousness, and unguided consciousness will lead to self-destruction.

There are many levels of happiness, some of which can be instantly gratified by establishing dominance, by consumption of materials goods, or by worshiping a religion. Nevertheless, true happiness is simply achieved by letting go of all desires, and by allowing the consciousness to accept and balance the opposing forces in everything. For example, to understand joy, one must also understand pain or suffering.

As simple as it may seem, most individuals are still in the stage of attaining happiness, with little thought to the influencing forces from the stage of immortality and ultimately the stage of divine wisdom.

Immortality

"The second stage is the Race to Immortality, which is an eternal state of being designed to be seductive, deceptive, and fatally competitive in the process of creating a lifeform capable of enduring all forces of destruction."

Immortality is an eternal state of being in which a universal pattern emerges that focuses on the cycle of birth and death.

Subconsciously ingrained in all lifeforms is the instinct to procreate by any means and to transfer its own genetic code to the next generation for a piece of immortality. Some processes are seductively cooperative while others are deceptive and fatally competitive. Procreation extends beyond the traditional reproductive process of gender selection into areas of asexual reproduction, cloning, metamorphosis, mutation, etc.

The tools and the technology are available today to engineer, biologically or mechanically, any species to better adapt to its environment, and its lifespan will continuously increase to the point of immortality.

Every cell and molecule and its infinitesimal parts in a lifeform is an individual sentient being with its own capabilities and contributions. Each cell and molecule acts as a repository of the ever-evolving instructions to re-build the physical traits of the inhabited lifeform. The cells and molecules are constantly making new connections with one another in a relentless effort to accumulate and retain awareness, as well as to collectively procreate to transfer the awareness amassed to the next generation before death arrives.

Death in itself is a stage of procreation in which bonded cells and molecules in a lifeform, and the unique consciousness, knowledge, and memory they attained are dissolved and are recycled to construct another lifeform. This stage is a form of re-incarnation in which various cells and molecules from previous lifeforms give rise to another lifeform with its own unique consciousness, building on previous awareness. At birth, the unique consciousness begins tracing a new path. At death, the unique consciousness disperses in preparation for a new path. Death signifies that the recent path to immortality is insufficient or a dead-end.

In the race to immortality, driven by hunger and the will to survive, all beings have equal privileges for harvesting one another for energy and resources, thus building upon past and existing knowledge via the selective process of evolution. Immortality is about engineering a lifeform of energy or matter which will house the collective consciousness that can endure all forces of destruction.

Divine Wisdom

"The third stage is the Quest for Divine Wisdom, which is an ambivalent state that entails continuous discovery for the knowledge

of everything, beyond contradicting beliefs, beyond the endless cycle, and beyond infinity."

Divine wisdom is in a state of ambivalence because existing beliefs are flawed by contradictions in words and languages. Thoughts are limited by the vocabularies of languages that are learned. All languages have contradictions, including the universal language of math. Math relies upon the concept of infinity, in which there is no final origin or destination. Therefore, a mind with limited awareness is trapped in an infinite loop of light, space, time, energy, and matter, searching for the code to exit.

In the known dimensions of space and time, the mind and senses are conditioned within the forces of electricity, magnetism, nuclear, and gravity. The human body currently contains the senses of sight, hearing, taste, smell, and touch. Sight allows for color, shape, and sharpness. Hearing allows for tone. Taste allows for flavor. Smell allows for scent. Touch allows for the sensation of temperature, texture, and movement. To date, all of our senses have been artificially enhanced or amplified by technology. For example, sight has been enhanced through the use of optical technology to view light in various wavelengths and peripherally to 360 degrees. Hearing has been enhanced through the use of telecommunication technology to listen to various radio frequencies. Taste and smell have been enhanced through the use of gas and chemical detectors to detect molecules and odors from extended distances. Touch has been enhanced through the use of various protective gears, remote controls, powered equipment, etc.

In addition, computer programs that interpret statistical patterns to simulate and even predict future events have enhanced the sixth sense of Extra Sensory Perception (ESP). The senses provide the perception of reality and as the senses change, so does reality. One's perception of reality is an elaborate reconstruction of information collected from the different senses. The information arrives at the brain at different times and it is processed in different places and at different speeds. Some realities are shared while others are individualized or self-deceiving.

Divine wisdom is about attaining knowledge and understanding of everything. In order to begin understanding everything, the naked senses need to be significantly amplified to detect all the hidden worlds and dimensions. Doing so raises the level of awareness, allowing the mind to visualize beyond its current plane of existence, beyond the endless cycle, and beyond infinity. As is, life is an illusion restricted only by our imagination. Reality can not realize what the mind can not conceive.

In the search for divine wisdom, some paths have been established and are being extended while other paths are being built and are littered with trials and tribulations. Eventually, all paths will converge, leading to divine wisdom. Until then, contradictions, endless cycles, and the answer to the question of what lay beyond infinity continue to be elusive.

The Meaning of Existence

"The paths to Happiness and Immortality are deeply intertwined, and are conceptually enhanced by the mirage of a civilization's lifestyles and cultures, as well as providing the foundation to the quest for Divine Wisdom. The answer is there, waiting to be extrapolated, in which process time is irrelevant."

Everyday, every society is conditioned by messages in the medium promoting its lifestyles and cultures. The existence of a society's lifestyles and cultures is to provide the illusion of comfort and security in order to develop the resources needed for the quest of happiness, immortality, and divine wisdom. Society changes over time and so do lifestyles, cultures, and the beliefs it creates to ensure survival. Lifeforms are designed to participate in the process of achieving happiness, immortality, and ultimately divine wisdom, all of which are the driving forces behind the changes in society.

Time is relevant, for a process takes time to build. However, once the knowledge is attained, time becomes irrelevant. The answer to every question has always been there. It is a matter of continuously improving the process to reduce the time it takes to find the answer. For example, when a problem is presented to a group to be solved, one person could solve the problem in one second, while another person could take millions of years to solve it. Therefore, the answer can come at anytime, from anywhere, by anyone.

To begin understanding the meaning of existence, life must be examined from a point of view beyond known dimensions, beyond death, and beyond the selfish perception that Earth and the human species are the center of creation. Life is not an accident, but an experiment to benefit its creator with only one purpose. In other words, all lifeforms are trapped in the same infinite loop as their creator. The creator endowed to life a piece of its own consciousness, similar to human's creation of artificial intelligence, to be utilized in the search for Divine Wisdom or the knowledge and understanding of everything.

Barring unforeseen forces, all sentient beings are caught in the same swirling river of the infinite loop. Similar to a lottery game, the sequences of events may appear random. However, all numbers, patterns or combinations of sequences are already predetermined, waiting to be extrapolated or re-extrapolated. Consequently, the Meaning of Existence for all lifeforms is simply to attain Divine Wisdom by revealing the patterns of creation to find the code to exit the infinite loop. Time is only relevant before the unique consciousness, knowledge, and memory attained is lost to the forces of death and destruction.

The laws of nature are already established in a closed system of the infinite loop. Nevertheless, the future is uncharted beyond the infinite loop, awaiting the power of imagination…

Again, I found myself in another paradox. I posed a question to myself. Does infinity exist and what is beyond infinity? In trying to answer my own question, I found that in terms of the looping of light, space, time, energy, and matter, infinity does exist. It is trapped in a rotating Universe of endless cycles and recurring patterns.

What I found even more puzzling is that 'Everything came from Nothing.' For example, the infinite loop '∞' arises from our perception of the number 'Zero' or the word 'Nothing.' From a scientific view in terms of energy, when positive energy (matter) is combined with negative energy (gravity), the result is Zero energy. In an abstract way, Zero or Nothing does exist because 'Everything came from Nothing.'

Ironically, Zero is the symbol of perfection, a sign of complete balance.

What lies beyond infinity? Because of the paradoxes inhibited in our limited forms of expression in languages, math, art, and music, that answer remains elusive. The paradox turned full circle again.

I posed another question to myself. What is time and is it possible to time travel? Our entire existence is governed by time, yet I found that time is an illusion. Our awareness and consciousness of the changes in things created this illusion.

The concept of time is a 'human invention' and relevant only as a point of reference, a measurement of an interval from point A to point B. When assessing time, we have been conditioned to think in terms of the past, the present, and the future. However, there is no past, no future. There is only the present. You could say that the future is a projection of the past but we are still in the here and now.

Is time travel possible? Many famous scientists believe that time travel is possible, including Einstein who introduced the idea that time was more like a river, speeding up and slowing down as it encounters gravitational field of a passing star or planet. The river of time can have whirlpools that close in on themselves, creating a time loop that could eventually come back to the original spot but displaced in time. One second on Earth is different from one second on the Moon or Mars. In fact, a clock on the Moon beats slightly faster than a clock on Earth. On Earth, a clock at the equator ticks faster than another in North America. Time passes more quickly when gravity is reduced.

Here's my perspective on this theory of time travel. A clock is made of matter to measure intervals of time. Matter behaves differently at different speeds, temperature and gravity. So the clock can be altered. Nevertheless, this version of time travel is full of paradoxes caught in an endless loop. For example, if you go back in time before you are born, you can not exist. It's the chicken and egg paradox of which came first.

I have my own theory of time travel that is slightly different and much easier to understand. As I mentioned before, time is an illusion. Time travel is nothing more than arranging or the rearranging of matter to a period in time that you want to create or recreate. Then by installing the finishing human touch of culture and beliefs for that period in time, you have traveled through time, which we have already done many times in the magic of movies.

For a simpler explanation of time travel, visualize for a moment a Rubik's cube with solid colors on all six faces. Let's say the faces of the colors represent the past. Now rotate the cubes and scramble the individual boxes till all the colors are mixed to represent the present. Then rotate the cubes again till all faces are returned back to the solid colors. You have just time traveled back to the past.

I think the reason why time travel is so appealing to many is simply because we think we have an advantage in bringing the knowledge attained from the past back to the past, or to be correct in predicting the future. It's a bit self serving as we all want to change the past or project the future to our advantage. Instead of trying to relive the past or predict the future, we can create our own future here and now!

In the past few centuries, science and technology have dismantled countless myths, including the old beliefs that the World is flat and Earth is the center of the Universe. Yet, we have produced even more questions than answers in our search for the truth, replacing one mystery with another. Science and technology have released us from the chain of organized religion, but it is only a tool not the answer itself. The answer to what we seek lies within our own imagination. It is our imagination that creates reality and that reality will continue to be challenged by science and religion.

The ultimate paradox is trying to use logic to explain an illogical world. I am left to conclude that the search for God and spirituality is a matter of individual faith, driven by our own imagination. Is this insane or genius?

Occasionally, I'm approached by friends and acquaintances seeking their own answers, yearning for wisdom from doors which I've walked through. Often, I had to contemplate whether they are ready to open those doors to attain a higher level of awareness. The ability to move among realities should only be traveled by the fearless, as the line between genius and insanity is quite blurred. If you are easily overwhelmed by fear, then you may not be able to bring yourself back to the reality of your choice. Time and again, my instinct tells me those doors are best left closed.

There is an old saying, "*When the student is ready, the teacher will appear.*"

Finding Balance

> ***"I think therefore I am"***
>
> -- Rene Descartes --

I've traveled to many places and met many interesting characters in my journey. It seems that they all have something in common. That common ground is the need to belong and to be connected. I often find that most people are off-balance and clueless on how to center or re-center themselves to achieve their dreams. I keep hearing the same rhetoric about life that we are here for a reason or things happen for a reason. I believe that even though there are contributing factors beyond our control that influence our decisions, in the end, we are accountable for our own actions. We are where we are because of the choices that we've made. If you don't like where you are make a change!

TEN LESSONS LEARNED FROM MY JOURNEY THUS FAR:

"Nothing lasts forever, as there is only one constant, and that is change"

"Life is a game, when your number is up, the game is over"

"Moderation is the key to health and happiness"

"No one has a real clue what life is all about"

"Common sense is not very common"

"Life is an illusion of the senses"

"No one controls free will, not even God"

"Death is the only thing that is certain in life"

"Words are meaningless until they are put into actions"

"Imagination is the most powerful gift ever given, but often neglected"

LIVING IN PARADOX

I have learned that change is the only constant in life. Every time I thought I have figured something out, it changes. As the paradox changes, I'm often confused and in constant struggle between personal beliefs and what society dictates as normal. What was once good is now evil and vice versa. For example, during previous wars, Germany, Japan, Russia, China, and Vietnam were considered evil empires. Today, they are called allies and trading partners. Franklin D. Roosevelt once said, "*The only thing we have to fear is fear itself.*" Truly, the enemy is within us. All we need is to find a common ground to overcome our fear, to change our mindset, to challenge our perspective, to find that balance within the paradox.

As time passed, I have learned to adapt to change and taught myself to recognize and understand how paradoxes work and the reason for them to exist. I began studying the meaning of symbolism. One such symbol is illustrated in the form of the Yin and Yang at the beginning of this chapter. Yin and Yang is the foundation that brings balance to the entire Universe. For Yin to exist, Yang must also exist. Contradiction is necessary because in order for something to exist, its opposite must also exist.

To understand one side, you also need to understand the other side. For example, in order to know Love, you need to know Hate. The same applies to Happiness and Sadness, Good and Evil, Reality and Illusion, etc. It is the contrast that allows us to distinguish the relationship of opposing forces, such as Positive and Negative, Light and Dark, Consciousness and Un-consciousness, Life and Death, etc.

You do not need to venture very far to understand this concept of living in paradox and the role it plays in our lives. Take the paradox of life and death as an example. If you spend much time in a hospital, you will understand the cycle of life and death, as it is played out there every hour. To know life, one has to know death, as death is the only thing that is certain in life. In a recent article in *Discover* magazine regarding death, it was estimated that 100 billion people have died since humanity began. In addition, it is almost impossible to approximate all lifeforms that have perished since the dawn of evolution. There is no getting around death. Learn to 'embrace' both life and death. Then plan your life and death accordingly. Death is simply the end of the cycle of life where we will be reborn in another form, spiritually or physically. In essence, we are already immortal, and immortality is the center in understanding the paradox of life and death.

In this world of contradiction, we need to be aware of these paradoxes. We need to learn to sort through the chaos and filter out the background noise to distinguish decisions that will bring meaning and purpose instead of false hope. No matter how complex something may seem, underlying all chaos is a simple order waiting to be discovered.

Living in a paradoxical world, we often walk on both sides of the road and confuse ourselves when things don't work out the way that we want them to be. It's a fine line that we cross every time we make a decision, going back and forth. But we don't seem to learn from our mistakes, as we continue to look for the magic pill to make us happy, for instant gratification to make life more bearable. We tend to drown ourselves in much drama, we take things for granted and often look for someone to blame for our own misery. This is a prison of our own making.

As the tension of unrealistic expectations in daily living mounts, there seems to be a direct correlation to the increasing rate of alcohol and drug abuse, as well as abuse of prescribed medications used as a form of counter action. The tension in our society is so fragile that a research group was able to predict the rate of domestic violence in a city by just monitoring the success or failure of local sports teams.

LIVING IN PARADOX

In a recent report from the National Institute on Drug Abuse (NIDA), one in four people in this country are addicted to some form of antidepressants, pain killers, and sleeping pills. This form of self medication is rising at an alarming rate. Unfortunately, all drugs become ineffective over time as the cells in our body mutate to adapt to the environment which will increase the demand for even more drugs to alleviate our pain and suffering. People today are more afflicted than ever with hypertension, high blood pressure, cancer, obesity, and unhealthy lifestyle-related diseases.

I believe most of our problems are self-inflicted or self-induced, resulting from fear, ignorance, greed, and plain old laziness.

Have we gone too far in domesticating ourselves? By definition, domestication is the process of genetically adapting an animal or plant to better suit the needs of human beings, yet we seem to have domesticated and disconnected ourselves from nature, mentally and physically. We live in a sterile society where everything is automated, processed, and packaged neatly to be delivered to our door mat. We contribute little or nothing, yet we believe we are entitled to all the benefits the world has to offer, wanting more, and more. Our thirst for satisfaction is never fulfilled, often leading to the fatalistic attitude of 'I don't care.' Are these traits of greed and laziness applicable to only humans, or life in general?

A few years ago, I read about an experiment on a species of bacteria that perished because they forgot how to feed themselves. Initially, this was a group of bacteria observed to be making their own protein as a food source. At the outset, researchers hand-fed the bacteria to cultivate and expand the colony for various tests. The bacteria colony thrived for months but when the researchers stop feeding the bacteria, they all began to die of starvation. It seems that after a few generations of being hand-fed, they got lazy and lost the ability to produce their own food. This experiment goes a long way to the saying, "*use it or lose it.*" Eventually, nature will discard what is not being used.

The human body too is a powerful protein producing chemical factory but 95% of our gene is not activated. Maybe that is why 95% of our brain is inactive. If we are to avoid the same fate as those bacteria, we are going to need to train or retrain ourselves the basic skills of life. This is the awakening process to be curious again.

We are not going to be able to solve all the problems in the world anytime soon. Nevertheless, gradually we can begin tackling one problem at a time, starting with our core beliefs.

Belief is one of the most powerful tools available for curing any ailments. In a study on the effect of placebo, according to Dr. Irving Kirsch, a psychologist at the University of Connecticut, *"The effectiveness of Prozac and similar drugs may be attributed almost entirely to the placebo effect, a fake or sugar pill."* His team analyzed 19 clinical trials of antidepressants and concluded that the expectation of improvement accounted for 75 percent of the drug's effectiveness. "*The critical factor*," says Kirsch, "*is our belief about what's going to happen to us. You don't have to rely on drugs to see profound transformation*." In an earlier study, his colleague analyzed 39 studies, conducted between 1974 and 1995, of depressed patients treated with drugs and psychotherapy, and they found that 50 percent of the drug effect is due to the placebo response.

Furthermore, in a recent article on *MSNBC.com* entitled, '*Placebo's power goes beyond the mind*,' using PET scanners and MRIs to peer into the heads of patients who respond to sugar pills, researchers have discovered that the placebo effect is not 'all in patients' heads' but rather in their brains. New research shows that belief in a dummy treatment leads to changes in brain chemistry. The reports demonstrate that anticipation of relief from a placebo can lead to an actual easing of aches when the brain makes more of its own pain-dousing opiates. Brain scans of patients show increases in a chemical messenger called dopamine which leads to an improvement in symptoms when patients think mistakenly that they are receiving real therapy.

The study took an extra step. The researchers rigged up an MRI so that people could watch real-time images of their brains while lying in the scanner. "*The idea was to use the images to teach study volunteers to consciously pump up activity in parts of the brain activated by the placebo effect*," says Dr. Sean Mackey, Director of Stanford's Neuro-imaging and Pain lab. "*Pain is not in the muscles or the arm that may be injured*," Mackey says, "*The pain is in our brains*." A signal starts out at an injured site and travels up to the brain, Mackey explains. But until the brain interprets that electrical signal, you don't actually 'feel' pain. Through trials and errors, volunteers were able to determine which kinds of thoughts fired up and turned down the brain regions linked to the pain.

The mind and brain have much more control over the body than we can voluntarily apply. Our body is already a powerful drug producing machine driven by the immune system. The immune system affects our ability to fend off illnesses like the common colds, the flu, and other viruses. It even protects us against heart disease and cancer. By controlling the brain, we can release chemicals to elevate mood, lower pain, eradicate diseases, increase concentration, improve memory, etc. Thus, a person's attitude and belief is essential to their mental, physical, and spiritual well-being. Don't underestimate your 'will power' to keep your immune system stimulated.

To better understand why so many people are struggling to find balance in their life, let's refer to the work of psychologist

Abraham Maslow and his theory of the Hierarchy of Needs. In his theory, he emphasized the importance of self-actualization, which is a process of growing and developing as a person and fulfilling your potential.

Maslow's Hierarchy of needs begin with:

Physiological Needs

These are the basic needs of survival, including the need for food, water, air, sleep, etc. Maslow believed that these needs are the basic and instinctive needs in the hierarchy because all needs are secondary until these physiological needs are met.

Security Needs

These are needs for safety and security. Security needs are important for survival but are not as primary as the physiological needs. Examples of security needs include a desire to earn an income, be healthy, and to be sheltered in a safe environment.

Social Needs

These are the needs for belonging, love, and affection. Relationships such as friendships, romantic attachments, and families help fulfill this need for companionship and acceptance. So does involvement in social, community, or religious groups.

Esteem Needs

Once satisfied with the first three needs, esteem needs becomes increasingly important. This is the need for self-esteem, personal worth, social recognition, and accomplishment.

Self-actualizing Needs

The highest level of Maslow's hierarchy of needs is self-actualizing, where a person becomes self-aware and more concerned with personal growth than concerned with the opinions of others, and they are more interested in fulfilling their potential.

Maslow believed that these needs are similar to instincts and play a major role in motivating human behavior. Maslow defined the highest-level of the pyramid to be a need for self-actualization, stemming from a desire to grow as a person. Physiological, security, social, and esteem needs are needs arising out of deprivation. Satisfying these lower-level needs is also important in order to avoid unpleasant feelings and to defy the genetically coded tendency for self-destruction.

Most of us are still having difficulty recognizing which stages we are in, thereby we continue to struggle to find balance between the five different levels of needs. Maslow's hierarchy of needs is just one small but important fragment of a much larger picture of life. To see the full picture, it is necessary to make the choices presented to fulfill these needs.

Life is a series of choices to fulfill our needs. If you're perfectly centered, then there is no need to make any more choices. But most of us are not centered. Albert Einstein once said, "*Life is like riding a bicycle, keep moving because if you stop, you will fall down.*" By constantly moving, you are balanced, and therefore you've found the center. Keep in mind, the center is not a single spot but a zone. If you have ever played sports or competed in anything, then you would have a better understanding of what the zone is. The zone that I'm referring to is when everything is in slow motion and you're still in control.

To find balance is to find the center of each paradox.

For example, the center for black and white is grey. The center for consciousness and un-consciousness is sub-consciousness. The center for fat and skinny is toned. The center for rich and poor is comfortable. Even a circle has a center and that is the midpoint of the diameter. The compromising ground is where you will find the happy medium for all paradoxes. This concept is somewhat simple to explain but much more difficult to practice, unless you are in touch with your senses.

There are five tools that we have already been given to find balance. Those tools are our senses. We learn about the world through our five physical senses to see, hear, feel, taste, and smell. The sense of sight helps us recognize our surroundings via color, motion, and distance. The sense of hearing helps us by focusing in on sound waves. The sense of touch helps us learn via the feeling of the texture, size and shapes. Taste helps us determine whether something is sweet, sour, salty, bitter, or a combination thereof. The sense of smell helps us to detect the gases in the air to determine whether the scents are healthy or harmful.

Nowadays, all these basic senses are more enhanced with technologies to better guide us to find the center of balance in our own universe. With a push of the button, we can now communicate across the world on a cellular phone or a web camera. Technological advancements have even allowed us to be in contact with probes and satellites in the deepest of oceans, across the solar system and beyond. We are now able to pierce deeper than ever in the micro and macro universe, unveiling lifeforms, structures, stars, and galaxies that were once thought impossible to exist.

There is one more sense that is often neglected and that is our sixth sense, or intuition. Intuition is the sense of the unseen world, a world that our physical senses can not detect. The sixth sense is the ability to tune in your own frequency, the frequency of those around you in this world or in the spiritual world, much like tuning in a radio or television channel. In the realm of the sixth sense, technology has not yet reached its full potential. Still, the most powerful tool to enhance it has existed since beginning of time, it is your imagination!

Imagine how your reality would change if you could hear more, see more, taste more, smell more, feel more, and you have control of the dial to turn those senses on and off at any volume at any given moment. What if you could record and transfer your memory. In an article on *CNN.com* entitled, '*Scientists test first human cyborg*,' Professor Kevin Warwick at the University of Reading, England, became the world's first cyborg - part human, part machine. Dr. Warwick carried out a series of pioneering experiments involving the neuro-surgical implantation of a device into the median nerves of his left arm in order to link his nervous system directly to a computer. If this phase succeeds with no complications, a similar device will be implanted in his wife. This will allow the investigation of how movement, thought or emotion signals could be transmitted from one person to the other, possibly via the Internet.

As more technologies become available to the masses, our senses will continue to be enhanced and our view of reality will again change. The question now is how to tap into your subconscious to activate your imagination to find a happy medium where balance resides.

A few years ago, out of curiosity, I became certified in Neuro Linguistic Programming (NLP), also referred to as self-hypnosis. NLP is a set of behavioral tools and techniques to allow you to change, adopt or eliminate behaviors, as you desire. It gives you the ability to choose your mental, emotional, and physical states of well-being. NLP begins by awakening the senses to give you insights into language and communication techniques, verbal and nonverbal. While in this state of intense relaxation and concentration of the senses, you can program the mind to consistently achieve the specific outcomes. NLP lets you re-program beliefs, behaviors, habits and emotions that reside in the subconscious.

I was skeptical at first due to the misconception that hypnosis is nothing more that a form of entertainment seen on stage and television. But after a few months of research it was clear how powerful subconscious suggestions can be. The subconscious is a layer in the mind that is on 'autopilot' reacting according to the principle that it seeks to avoid unwanted feelings and to obtain pleasure for the sake of survival, regardless of the consequence. The subconscious is also home to emotions, imagination, memories, and the autonomous nervous system which controls our physical well-being.

In other words the mind affects the body and the body affects the mind. The subconscious is very good at dealing with many complex instructions but it needs an occasional reprogramming to find balance.

Examples of problems solved through NLP or hypnosis include weight control, smoking control, drug and alcohol therapy, gambling addiction, stress management, self-image, healing of the physical body, etc. Furthermore, we have been conditioned by NLP for years by our friends, families, teachers, peers, and the media. Media outlets such as newspaper, radio and television advertising are also using NLP to try to persuade us to do things or buy a particular product. They constantly bombard us with repetitive messages to reinforce a suggestion. If you have ever found yourself at the checkout register not knowing why you put something in your shopping basket, you have just experienced NLP.

Further evidence that the mind is programmable can be found in a recent study on mind control at the University of Pittsburgh. A monkey's real arms were restrained in plastic tubes, and electrodes were attached to its region of the brain responsible for voluntary movement. Using food as a motivator, the monkey was taught to feed itself using a robotic arm electronically linked to its brain. In similar studies at various universities, monkeys were taught to use their thoughts to play computer games and move objects around the room with wireless sensors.

If a monkey can be taught to tap into its own sensory and consciousness to control its environment, then we can also teach ourselves to use our senses to adapt to our environment.

We learn best about our world when we use all our senses simultaneously. If one sense is inhibited, the other ones will compensate. The brain is programmable and it is constantly being rewired based upon the input from the senses to get things done. The brain just needs motivation for neurons to be connected to activate both sides of the hemisphere. Find activities that will utilize all your senses to awaken them to their fullest potential.

There are many things you can do to stimulate your senses. You can create your own list to include cooking, dining, meditation, intimacy, music, art, movies, reading, adventure sports, etc. Do anything that will stimulate the senses and all for the better if you can stimulate those senses in tandem.

One of my favorite methods to stimulate my senses is to indulge myself in a foreign culture. Culture is a form of human expression and a way of life of a society. It includes codes of manners, dress, language, religion, rituals, food, drinks, behaviors and systems of belief. When exploring a culture, I have no choice but to use all my senses, especially when I'm traveling in that country.

Another favorite indulgent of the senses for me is sleep. Scientists are still trying to figure out why we sleep and dream, and if it is necessary for human beings or for any species. Perhaps, it is to recharge and repair the body, encode memories collected for the day, improve recall ability, or make neuronal connections.

For me, I enjoy sleeping not for the sake of sleeping but to dream. I figure if I'm going to sleep more than one third of my life away, I might as well put the sleep to good use. In dreams, I'm able to digest information collected throughout the day to establish meaningful patterns as to what to expect in the future.

Over the years, I have learned how to lucid dream. As in NLP, I programmed myself with "repetitive messages" to strengthen my belief to reinforce the dream I'm trying to achieve. With practice, I was able to control my dreams to change the scene or situation, and be in control of my own actions.

Sleep time is a great way to solve problems and to expand your imagination. There is no boundary in dreams. Dare to imagine and see how far you can push your senses. In order to be successful at controlling your dreams you have to "believe it is possible", just like in real life.

Live, experience, and visualize beyond your wildest imagination. Vincent Van Gogh once said, "*I dream my painting, then I paint my dream.*" The only reason anything exists is because someone conjured it in their mind. Once the idea is shared and acted upon, it will then materialize into a reality.

LIVING IN PARADOX

In essence, life is an illusion, a perception of the senses as it is our senses that determine what is real. Beware that reality changes from one society to another. Reality depends on the collective consciousness of what the society has agreed upon at that moment in time to be real. That universally accepted reality may not coincide with your version of reality.

No one has a real clue of what life is all about and we are just feeding off each other's ideas and interpretations. Your own reality is only limited by your imagination, the most powerful gift ever given. This gift of self awareness, when your senses are at their peak, will always help you in the quest for balance.

In order to find balance within our paradoxical world, your belief system will need to change accordingly to adapt to the environment.

There is an old saying, *"When in Rome, do as the Romans do."*

Next Steps

> ***"All organisms with complex nervous systems are faced with the moment-to-moment question that is posed by life: What shall I do next?"***
>
> -- Sue Rumbaugh and Roger Lewin --

So here I am again, a chameleon at a crossroad, pondering the choices and knowledge accumulated, wondering where my next adventure lies.

On a recent trip to Seattle, Washington, I was asking directions on a bus from a man standing next to me. As it turns out, he is one of the founders of a small internet company named '43 Things,' funded by Amazon.com. 43 Things was formed on the premise that 43 is the right number of things for a busy person to try to achieve in life. We all have goals but most of us never get around to making a list. 43 Things can help you document your success, share information, and make progress on what matters to you most. Thus, I began implementing my own list, 10 things at a time.

TEN THINGS I WANT TO DO NEXT:

"Live more consciously and continue to look for universal patterns"

"Study neuroscience, neuro-linguistic programming, and magic"

"Spend more quality time with my kids"

"Learn to speak Mandarin"

"Learn how to cook"

"Write six more books"

"Renew my love for martial arts"

"Sign up for inner space and outer space exploration"

"Identify another technological breakthrough that would benefit society"

"Travel more: Per St. Augustine, the philosopher - the world is a book, and those who don't travel, only read one page"

LIVING IN PARADOX

One of the top ten things I wanted to do next was completed in September 2006. I finally made a complete circle and took a trip to Vietnam. It was my first visit in 31 years since the Vietnam War ended.

With only two weeks allotted, I visited Ho Chi Minh City, Hue, and Hanoi. Ho Chi Minh City (aka Saigon) was the former capital of South Vietnam, Hue was the ancient capital of Vietnam, and Ha Noi was the former capital of North Vietnam and is now the capital of Vietnam.

As soon as I landed in Ho Chi Minh City I was quickly overwhelmed with the noise and traffic from thousands of mopeds. Ho Chi Minh is a city of roughly eight million inhabitants and there seems to be just as many mopeds as there are people. Initially, I felt a bit odd as everyone kept staring at me since most Vietnamese are shorter than I am. I could hear them talking about me when I walked by as they wondered aloud about my nationality. Then, they were surprised when they heard me speak. Overall, the people are very genuine and overly accommodating.

My biggest challenge in the first few days was to learn how to cross the street in the endless flow of traffic. In one instance, I recorded a video of a blind man crossing a major intersection by himself. If a blind man can do it, so can I. It was pretty scary at first but the key to crossing the streets was to dive right in with no hesitation, as the cars and mopeds automatically swirled around me.

Like any sprawling metropolis, Ha Noi and Ho Chi Minh City is noisy, crowded, and filled with street vendors and open markets, but that's the charm of big cities. However, the landscape changes dramatically once I left the city limits to encroach on the countryside. The country is more beautiful and exotic than I remembered. I saw part of Vietnam that was forbidden during war time such as the remote villages and the northern part of Vietnam. The countryside is lined with fruit trees, rice fields, and water buffalos. The merging of mountains, flatlands, rivers, beaches, and islands is more picturesque than words can describe.

On this trip, I was very fortunate to be able to experience both the VIP and backpacker tours. One day I'm in a five-star hotel and the next day I'm in a two-star hotel mingling with street vendors. I also found out that there is a major advantage in knowing the language, since Vietnamese and Vietnamese speaking individuals get a discount price on most everything. I met people from all over the world such as Australia, England, Holland, Germany, China, France, Japan, Thailand, etc. However, it was a bit odd that I did not meet anyone from America.

The most memorable part of my trip was riding on the back seat of a moped weaving through the traffic of Ho Chi Minh City in the pouring rain. There were many more memories collected and recalled during my time in Vietnam, but in retrospect I didn't feel fully connected with the country and its people. I think it's because I was traveling in the prism of an American tourist. A few photos from my trip are attached in the following pages.

Photo 28, Top: The road to Hanoi. The past is left behind to give way to Vietnam's integration into the world economy.

Photo 29, Bottom: The Metropolitan in Ho Chi Minh City. The emerging economy of Vietnam today.

Photo 30, Top: Traffic jam in the bubbling and dynamic City of Ho Chi Minh, driven by a young and promising generation.

Photo 31, Bottom: On the way to the marketplace. The relentless will to overcome poverty supported by instinctive entrepreneurship.

LIVING IN PARADOX

Today, Vietnam is a young and vibrant country whose people are always on the move. The median age is only 26 years old. The majority of the population seems so occupied with making a living and overcoming poverty that they have no time left to focus on trivial and superficial things. The people are extremely hard-working and purely rely on their instinctive surviving skills and relentless determination to achieve a better future for themselves and the next generation.

Poverty, as a percent of the population, has declined significantly and is now lower than that of China and India. Similar to China, Vietnam is quickly moving from a developing country to an emerging country. That was quite evident when I visited my old house in Ho Chi Minh City. The once scenic view of the canal behind our home is now replaced with highrise condominums.

According to data from *Vietpartners.com*, from 1995-2005, Vietnam attracted over $40 billion from foreign direct investment. The government has relentlessly perfected its legal system, created more incentive policies for foreign investors to fulfill its commitments to the international community.

Economically, Vietnam is the star of Southeast Asia, growing at 8% and projected to grow another 8% in 2007. The high growth rate has contributed to a strong business environment and membership in the World Trade Organization is scheduled for December of 2006.

At the moment, Vietnam is at the center of a paradox, leveraging technology to leap-frog itself out of poverty, directly into a modern society. My instinct tells me that I am going to be involved somewhere in this process.

In all, I look at life as an experiment, a trial run to see what I am capable of achieving. I want to make a conscious effort to leave the world a better place than when I found it. I hope to inspire more people to live each day passionately, with no fear and no regrets.

For this journey of life, time is limited. The Grim Reaper awaits. When your number is up, the game is over. Go on your own terms. How would you like to be remembered?

Whether you're looking for love, happiness, fame, fortune, power, or knowledge there is no one-size-fits-all magic formula. Passion is the key. Live your life every day with excitement. Reach for each goal with enthusiasm. Take the time to stop and reflect.

Success is a journey, not a destination, so stop running. Accept the temporary setbacks and failures. These are life's precious opportunities to learn and grow. Take the time and effort to find your own formula and your own destiny. Just as a postcard can not make you experience the destination, life can not be explained. It must be lived.

Leave your security blanket behind and make a list of ten things you want to do next. Develop a plan and begin your journey. Life is just a game, learn the rules, make new rules, enjoy the ride, and don't forget to smile!

> ***"Never take life seriously; nobody gets out alive anyway"***
>
> -- Anonymous --